S0-ASE-233

"Kevin Harney shows us that true strength comes in God's presence. When we feel weak, inadequate, disparaged, and powerless, God is ready, willing, and anxiously waiting to empower us. A fantastic read for daily meditation."

—**Mark Batterson**, *New York Times*
bestselling author of *The Circle Maker;*
lead pastor, National Community Church, Washington, DC

"I love this book. Each story takes me straight to the heart of Jesus and out into the world to serve him. As Harney writes, 'The empowered yield to the winds of the Holy Spirit. They hear the call of Jesus and follow.' It's the life (or adventure?) we're created to live!"

—**Nancy Grisham, PhD**, speaker; author of *Thriving*

"For many people on the journey of life, it feels like the energy grid has gone offline; the circuit breaker has flipped to 'off.' If you need a fresh infusion of hope, strength, and God's power in your life, then this book is for you. Walking through *Empowered by His Presence* will share the experiences of real people from the Bible, offering relevant wisdom to help you draw from God's presence in powerful and life-giving ways."

—**Rev. Dr. Tom DeVries**, general secretary
of the Reformed Church in America

"If you've been feeling a little overwhelmed by life, *Empowered by His Presence* is a must-read. You won't be disappointed. Kevin's words provide strength for the day and hope for tomorrow."

—**Dann Stouten**, pastor; author of *The Gate*

"Kevin Harney lives in the 'real world' and is gifted at helping the rest of us do just that—live for Christ and in his strength in the day to day. Take these thoughts and apply them to your everyday life!"

—**Dan Seaborn**, president and founder of Winning At Home, Inc.
(www.winningathome.com)

"Kevin Harney in *Empowered by His Presence* reveals the freeing reality of being empowered by God's presence and strength in fresh new ways. It cuts right to the core of what it means to be a true disciple of Jesus."

—**Wally Armstrong**, professional golfer, author, teacher

"Nothing inspires as well as old truths portrayed in fresh ways that compel. Kevin Harney uses a very engaging format to invite us to remember and pay attention to the things that matter to God and which were lived so well by his Son, Jesus. Now it is our turn to reflect the heart of God to a world that desperately needs to understand his relentless love for all people. After savoring Kevin's book over several weeks time, as he suggests, I am renewed and reminded, again, of my role in God's great restoration effort! It's a privilege I will pursue with even greater zeal following my time with *Empowered by His Presence*."

—**Scott W. Bolinder**, executive vice president, Biblica

"*Empowered by His Presence* is a clarion call to experience God's presence and power daily. Kevin Harney introduces you to Bible characters who tapped into God's always-available power source. You will journey with people like Abraham, Hannah, and Elijah and learn how to encounter God as they did. In the process you will gain much more: an overview of the Bible, a very doable four-week reading process, as well as resources that lift the book from merely something you read to something you do. I can't wait to use it with my small group and in my mentoring sessions. This book is genuinely life-transforming."

—**Rowland Forman**, mentor; director of Living Stones Ministries, Auckland, New Zealand; author of *The Lost Art of Lingering*

"I love and admire Kevin Harney. Kevin has been a personal friend for many years. He is one of the great Christian leaders in this country today. Kevin is a gifted pastor and author with an evangelist's heart. His unique ministry is an effective force for winning people to Christ and strengthening the local church. His commitment to God is more consistent and warm than most people I know. I love this book—it spoke to my soul and I believe it will be an energizing blessing to all who open their hearts to its message."

—**Wes Dupin**, founder and pastor of DaybreakChurch.tv

"Kevin has moved us beyond Sunday school stories to the real life, guts, fear, doubt, and faith of some of our biblical heroes. Reading this, I realized their issues were very contemporary for this day. In fact, this is a work that needs us to ponder it—to allow time for us to hear from God. Truly a book that speaks to the times in which we live. God wants to do 'Greater Things,' but we must be *Empowered by His Presence*. A must-read."

—**Jo Anne Lyon**, general superintendent, The Wesleyan Church

"Kevin Harney is a gifted pastor, teacher, writer, and friend. He lives his faith and encourages other to do so. His books have helped me know what it truly means to be connected to God and Jesus. *Empowered by His Presence* may be his best work. Kevin's clear insight of being powerful, powerless, or empowered really spoke to my heart. Each of us find ourselves at times being powerful or powerless on our own when in reality we need to be *empowered* by his presence in all circumstances. I plan to put this book to work in my life on a daily basis. When my twenty-one-year-old son Nick was called home to be with Jesus in heaven, my wife Betsy and I needed to be *empowered* by his presence to make it through each day. He was there. Kevin and his wife Sherry were also there with us to help us each step of the way."

—Terry Davis, CEO, Tri-California Events

"Everything I read by Kevin Harney inspires and impacts me in life-changing ways. He not only understands the challenges we all face, but in this new work he helps us access the power of God in the areas we need it most."

—Gene Appel, senior pastor, Eastside Christian Church, Anaheim, CA

"These powerful vignettes are for the worn and the weary, the disappointed and the discouraged. In *Empowered by His Presence*, Kevin Harney skillfully portrays the disrupted lives of a host of biblical characters. As we journey with them, we gain skill in living the empowered life. Savor this book."

—Jeff Manion, senior pastor, Ada Bible Church; author of *The Land Between* and *Satisfied*

"What I love about *Empowered by His Presence* is its livability. It's like you are eating dinner (Kevin prefers Mexican) at the table right there with Kevin. He shares about real life, real Bible people and the real Jesus. I urge you to taste and enjoy!"

—Bob Bouwer, senior pastor, Faith Church (multi-site), South Chicagoland–Northwest Indiana

"I consider Dr. Harney to be in the top 1 percent of pastor-theologians in North America in terms of spirituality, pastoral leadership, evangelism, and the development and growth of local congregations. All of us would do well to learn from him. He is solidly biblical, wonderfully creative, and refreshingly practical and down-to-earth. I read anything Kevin writes.

This volume is a wonderful spiritual guide for all those who want to love Jesus more deeply in their personal life and in their ministries. As I did with another of Dr. Harney's books some years ago, I plan to suggest this book to my bimonthly covenant Bible study group to which I have belonged for over twenty years. The book's final section on mission is itself worth the price of the book."

—Charles Van Engen, professor of Biblical Theology of Mission, School of Intercultural Studies, Fuller Theological Seminary

"Walk alongside some of the Bible's heroes and see the Scriptures come alive as Kevin Harney leads you to understand what really happened in some of the familiar stories of the Bible. This book is packed with biblical knowledge presented in a way that inspires and challenges the reader. That is how devotional material should be written."

—Ajith Fernando, teaching director, Youth for Christ, Sri Lanka

EMPOWERED

BY HIS PRESENCE

RECEIVING THE STRENGTH
YOU NEED EACH DAY

KEVIN G. HARNEY

BakerBooks

a division of Baker Publishing Group
Grand Rapids, Michigan

© 2014 by Kevin G. Harney

Published by Baker Books
a division of Baker Publishing Group
P.O. Box 6287, Grand Rapids, MI 49516-6287
www.bakerbooks.com

Printed in the United States of America

All rights reserved. No part of this publication may be reproduced, stored in a retrieval system, or transmitted in any form or by any means—for example, electronic, photocopy, recording—without the prior written permission of the publisher. The only exception is brief quotations in printed reviews.

Library of Congress Cataloging-in-Publication Data is on file at the Library of Congress, Washington, DC.

ISBN 978-0-8010-1469-7

Scripture quotations are from the Holy Bible, New International Version®. NIV®. Copyright © 1973, 1978, 1984, 2011 by Biblica, Inc.™ Used by permission of Zondervan. All rights reserved worldwide. www.zondervan.com

14 15 16 17 18 19 20   7 6 5 4 3 2 1

In keeping with biblical principles of creation stewardship, Baker Publishing Group advocates the responsible use of our natural resources. As a member of the Green Press Initiative, our company uses recycled paper when possible. The text paper of this book is composed in part of post-consumer waste.

This book is dedicated to ordinary people who long to be empowered so they can live an extraordinary life for the glory of God!

It is for the mother who walks through each day loving her children, wiping noses, teaching simple truths, asking a daughter for the thousandth time, "What do you say?" and praying that someday she will say "Thank you" unprompted. In your faithful weariness, God is ready to draw near and empower you for one more day.

It is for the office manager who does their job with intensity and excellence and wonders if anyone notices. Who puts in more hours than are counted and feels depleted, discouraged, unappreciated. God is ready to connect you to his sources of strength.

It is for the college student who does their homework, studies hard, gets good grades but wonders if there will be a job for them after graduation. God's power and hope are closer than you think.

It is for the pastor who pours out prayers, sermons, and care from a deep place of compassion and wonders if the reservoir is just about to run dry.

It is for the husband who works hard every day, seeks to care for his family, serves his community and church and wonders if he will have what it takes to do it again tomorrow.

I dedicate this book to everyday people who are ready to take the hand of God and watch his presence fill their heart, transform their life, and empower them to live for his glory today!

In other words, I dedicate this book to you.

Contents

Introduction: Powerful, Powerless, or Empowered?   13

SECTION 1:
Experiencing God's Presence in Suffering, Loss, and Pain

1. Job's Epic Story of Suffering: *When Relentless Suffering Meets Unyielding Faith*   21

2. Paul's 195 Scars: *Facing Abuse for Doing the Right Thing*   27

3. Hannah's Sorrow and Tears: *When Dreams Don't Come True*   33

4. Joseph's Journey of Loss: *Far from Home But Close to God*   39

5. Peter, a Disciple's Sacrifice: *Trading Everything for Jesus*   46

6. Jesus's Scream of Loneliness: *Our Example of Suffering with Purpose*   52

Resources for Living an Empowered Life   58

9

Contents

SECTION 2:
Encountering God in the Community of His People

7. A Paralytic and His Friends: *Are You on the Mat or Carrying It?* 69

8. Paul and Timothy: *Climbing in Community* 74

9. Ruth and Naomi: *Forging a Family* 80

10. Lois, Eunice, and Timothy: *The Blessing of a Spiritual Legacy* 86

11. The Woman at the Well: *From Outcast to Embraced* 94

12. Jesus and His Friends: *Crushed and Poured Out, But Not Alone* 101

Resources for Living an Empowered Life 107

SECTION 3:
Empowered for the Journey by Receiving God's Rest

13. God's Example: *Why Would God Take a Day Off?* 117

14. Moses's Teaching: *Called to Rest* 123

15. Israel's Struggle: *Resistance, Manna, and Maggots* 129

16. David's Shepherd Psalm: *Green Pastures and Still Waters* 134

17. Elijah's Turning Point: *The Value of a Nap and a Snack* 141

18. Jesus's Early Mornings: *Intimacy with the Father* 147

Resources for Living an Empowered Life 154

SECTION 4:
Propelled Onward by the Call and Mission of God

19. Paul's Call: *Knocked Down, Blinded, and Turned Around* 163

20. Isaiah's Invitation: *Speaking with Blistered Lips* 170

21. Abraham's Journey: *Going without Knowing* 177

22. Esther's Risk: *This Could Cost You Everything* 183

23. Mary's Maternity: *I Am the Lord's Servant* 189

24. Jesus's Mission: *Seeking and Saving the Lost* 195

Resources for Living an Empowered Life 201

Afterword: *Receiving the Strength I Need Today* 207

Small Group Discussion Guide 209

Notes 219

Introduction

Powerful, Powerless, or Empowered?

A close friend of mine is the president and CEO of a renewable power company. In the simplest terms, his company harnesses the energy of the sun and creates electricity. In a world looking for alternative energy sources, this is one great long-term option. Scientists have varied views on how long our sun will continue to warm the earth and give light and life. The best guesses range between one billion and nine billion years. If they are right, my friend's company seems to have a pretty good shelf life.

Entire nations and economies are built on energy reserves, power sources, and the availability of the fuel that keeps cars on the road, planes in the air, lights on at night, and heat available in the cold months of winter. Power is a driving force in our world. But, as important as this is, there is an even more urgent need. People today are looking for empowerment for the soul. Every follower of Jesus longs for sources of strength that don't fade away, or run out. We want to know, where can I receive strength as I seek to live another day?

The good news is that God has an endless supply of energy, power, and strength. His presence and love are the ultimate renewable power source because they never run out. He is ready to empower us to live each and every day for him.

Here is the dilemma. We often avoid or fail to notice the best power sources. Like the sun, they are around us and available each day, but their very presence can be missed by virtue of their familiarity. Some people forget that the God who is with them is the source of everything and anything they need. His very presence offers unlimited strength, hope, power, love, energy, and grace.

It is time for us to open our eyes, minds, and hearts to the power of God. We are not powerful in our own strength. If we seek to muster up our own might and muscle to make it through the journey of life, we will always fall short. Sadly, some people see themselves as powerless and focus only on their lack of strength. They don't even try to press through the challenges of following Jesus in this crazy world! What God offers and wants for us is an empowered life. This means plugging into his power sources each day.

Longing to Be Powerful

For many people, being powerful is the Promised Land! It is the place to which most human beings want to ascend, even if we won't admit it. Some earn this place and others inherit it. Authority, influence, cultural clout, and self-confidence mark the lives of these people. Powerful and self-made men and women seem to have it all and they know what to do with it.

We have all read the stories of a boy or girl who starts at the bottom and climbs to the top. They have worked hard, sacrificed, paid the price, and now they have arrived. They are powerful! Their life is practically perfect and their future seems unshakably secure.

This kind of life is precarious. Wealthy people have watched their fortune evaporate between the opening and closing bells of the stock exchange. Healthy people have been devastated with one doctor's report. Self-made people have been unmade by one bad choice. Being powerful in our own strength is like a mist that disappears when the sun rises. None of us has the power we need, in and of ourselves, to make it through all the challenges we face.

The Lie of Being Powerless

On the other end of the continuum are those who see themselves as powerless. They are victims, oppressed and discouraged. They have not pulled themselves up by their own proverbial bootstraps. Instead, they have no boots at all. They feel out of control and don't know what to do about it.

Our world has a growing number of people who see themselves as pawns on the chessboard of life and they see no way out. More and more people hold their hand out on street corners looking for someone to give them enough to make it through another day. An increasing number of people look to government agencies who play big brother and dole out more "entitlements" with each passing year. There is a whole generation of people who have learned that there are "haves" and "have-nots" in this world and somewhere along the way they decided that they are in the "have-not" column. They might not like it, but what can they do? They feel powerless.

These people don't even try to be powerful. Instead, they feel consigned to a powerless existence. They believe the lie that things are hopeless and there is no way their lot in life will change.

Getting By

Most of us live between these two poles. We walk the pathways of this life feeling neither powerless nor powerful. We simply live. We move from day to day and check things off our to-do lists, we work hard at our job so we can make ends meet, we have meaningful relationships, raise families, pay our bills, and make time to relax a bit on the weekend.

We top off our tank with enough fuel to manage our life for another week. In our quiet moments we wonder what it would feel like to have it all together, be confident in the future, and feel truly empowered. In our really quiet and introspective moments, we might say a quick prayer and ask God to keep us from tottering over the precipice and ending up in the valley of the powerless.

An Empowered Life

Do you feel powerful?

Do you see yourself as powerless?

Are you simply seeking to survive and make it through the next month, week, day, or hour?

What if there are sources of strength that God provides that will help you live an empowered life? What if the very presence of God provides the strength you need?

This book is for all those who long to discover the endless and life-giving sources of strength that are found when we walk in the presence of the God of the universe. It is for people who don't need to be in control of everything but also refuse to be victimized by this world. It is for ordinary people who long to be filled with the extraordinary and amazing power of the living God each and every moment.

In this book you will meet biblical characters who were surprised by the presence and power of God in times of pain, weariness, loneliness, and confusion. You will discover that God is ready to fill you with the power you need for the next step of your journey with him.

God is powerful but never predictable. His ways are not our ways. God is ready to empower you for the next leg of your voyage, but his strength is not always what you would expect. You must be humble and accept his delivery system. God is ready to provide the empowerment you need, but he will do it his way.

The Journey Ahead

This book is not meant to be rushed through. I invite you to read just one short chapter each day. If you do this, it will take four weeks to read this book. Each chapter tells the story of a real person from the pages of the Bible. Their story will reveal a distinct and helpful window into how God empowers people with his presence.

At the end of each chapter you will find a brief reading titled "From the Heart." What I seek to do in each of these reflections is capture the heartbeat of the biblical character and present the message God teaches us through their life.

I have also provided some Bible passages you can read that will teach you more about each character and their journey of being empowered by the presence of God.

Finally, at the end of each section of the book, you will find "Resources for Living an Empowered Life." These are creative and interactive materials to help you take steps forward in connecting with God and receiving his strength. A dear and godly woman who read this manuscript before it was published told me, "I planned to just quickly skim the resources at the end of the sections and focus on the chapters. But one night after I finished reading the first section, I woke up and could not get back to sleep. So I began to read and engage in the exercises provided at the end of section 1." She told me, "God spoke to me in powerful ways, I met with Jesus. And I felt his power filling me as I walked through the resources." I want to encourage you to take some time and use the materials at the end of each of the four parts of this book and see if God does the same for you.

For those who want to walk through *Empowered* with a small group or an entire congregation, you will find free small group resources, preaching materials, and other helpful tools provided on my website: kevingharney.com. You can order books and the *Empowered* DVD curriculum at a great discount on this site. There are also small group reflection questions in the back of this book.

I am praying that every person, small group, and congregation that walks through *Empowered* will experience the joy and freedom of being filled with God's strength and presence in fresh, new, daily ways!

Kevin Garth Harney

Experiencing God's Presence in Suffering, Loss, and Pain

Dear friends, do not be surprised at the fiery ordeal that has come on you to test you, as though something strange were happening to you. But rejoice inasmuch as you participate in the sufferings of Christ, so that you may be overjoyed when his glory is revealed.

1 Peter 4:12–13

And the God of all grace, who called you to his eternal glory in Christ, after you have suffered a little while, will himself restore you and make you strong, firm and steadfast. To him be the power for ever and ever. Amen.

1 Peter 5:10–11

1

Job's Epic Story of Suffering

When Relentless Suffering
Meets Unyielding Faith

"Naked I came from my mother's womb,
and naked I will depart.
The LORD gave and the LORD has taken away;
may the name of the LORD be praised."

In all this, Job did not sin by charging God with wrongdoing.

Job 1:21–22

To anyone who knew him well, Jerry had an idyllic life. A loving wife, great kids, a meaningful job, and a vibrant relationship with Jesus. He had ministered as a chaplain at a Christian college and had impacted the lives of many young people. He was now a teacher at another well-known Christian school. His life was not perfect, but let's say things were looking pretty good!

In one night, in the flash of a moment, with the crashing sound of metal on metal, everything changed. A drunk driver veered across the road and hit the van Jerry was driving. Before the night was over, Jerry Sittser was facing an entirely different life. His mother, wife, and one of his daughters were gone. Three generations of the women in Jerry's life were no longer in his life. He was now a widower. A single father. A new chapter of life was thrust on him with no warning or preparation.[1]

What do you do? What do you say? How do you respond to uninvited, unwanted, and unexpected tragedy?

Maybe it is best to start by speaking these words first uttered by a man named Job:

> Naked I came from my mother's womb,
> and naked I will depart.
> The LORD gave and the LORD has taken away;
> may the name of the LORD be praised. (Job 1:21)

Job was a man who had it all! Faith in God. A good, honorable, and upright heart. A wife and ten children. Wealth beyond measure. Time to celebrate and enjoy the good gifts from above. Friends to celebrate with. You get the picture . . . and the picture was close to perfect.

Why would a man with everything the world had to offer, a spiritually pure pedigree, and a passionate heart for God utter these words?

> Naked I came from my mother's womb,
> and naked I will depart.
> The LORD gave and the LORD has taken away;
> may the name of the LORD be praised. (Job 1:21)

Because, when the winds of change blew in the life of a man named Job, they blew with hurricane force. Warm, sunny, and calm days were replaced with heart-and-soul-splitting storms. In the blink of an eye his wealth evaporated, his workforce was decimated, and all of Job's children were killed. A freak storm hit the house where his beloved sons and daughters were feasting, the roof descended with crushing force, and their lives were snuffed out.[2]

When he received the news of all that had transpired, Job fell to the ground in worship and spoke these words. Read them slowly. Read them out loud. Let them sink into your soul:

> Naked I came from my mother's womb,
>   and naked I will depart.
> The LORD gave and the LORD has taken away;
>   may the name of the LORD be praised. (Job 1:21)

Suffering distills our faith to its purest elements. Anguish is the fire that refines us until we become pure gold. Pain pulls up a chair, sits toe-to-toe with us, gazes eye-to-eye and asks, "Do you really believe all you claim to believe about God?"

Do you want to see what your faith is made of? Are you ready to measure the resolve of your heart? Are you sure you believe God is sovereign and the risen Lord Jesus is on the throne of your life?

Just walk, or crawl, through a time of suffering.

When the doctor's report comes back and the news is crushing. When a loved one is teetering on the edge of life and death. When a child has wandered far from home and God. When the stock market free-falls. When the storms of life show no sign of letting up. This is when faith becomes real.

Don't check your pulse when you have been sitting on a lounge chair after relaxing for a few hours and sipping cold beverages. Instead, check it just after you have finished a triathlon.

What words come out of your mouth when suffering moves in like an uninvited relative and shows no sign of departing? What do you say when pain is not a surprise but a defining and familiar element of every step you take and every waking moment? What do people hear come out of your mouth when finances are uncertain, or absolutely certain in their absence? Does it sound anything like this?

> Naked I came from my mother's womb,
>   and naked I will depart.
> The LORD gave and the LORD has taken away;
>   may the name of the LORD be praised. (Job 1:21)

23

I had the privilege of getting to know Jerry Sittser when he came to speak at a pastors' gathering I hosted yearly at the church I served in Michigan. He had not remarried after that tragic crash but was raising his remaining children as a single dad. He read cookbooks regularly so he could prepare new meals for his family and teach them how to cook. He was both father and mother. Jerry was teaching full-time and parenting more than full-time. And he was not bitter. Jerry knew much of pain and loss, but his heart was still intact. He had power to live each day because the source of all power was living in him and filling him moment by moment . . . and he knew it.

As part of his healing process, Jerry wrote a book called *A Grace Disguised*. I have read it closely and given away dozens of copies through the years. One of the things I love about Jerry's outlook is that he is clear that we should not quantify suffering. Early in his journey of loss, people would say, "You are like Job! Your suffering is so great. What you experienced must be one of the worst experiences of suffering ever."

Jerry is always quick and gentle in letting people know that his suffering is exactly that—*his* suffering. And their suffering is theirs.

It is not wise to compare suffering. We ought not categorize suffering. We should certainly not act like our suffering is worse than what someone else has experienced. And we should not believe our pain is less significant.

Suffering is suffering. It is ours as we walk through it. It invariably leads to tears, sorrow, heartache, and struggle. It usually comes unannounced and we rarely know when it will leave.

Most of all, suffering can crush our faith or strengthen it. The decision is ours. Will I cling to Jesus through my pain and with tears streaming down my face? Or will I turn my back and walk away from the only One who can carry me through? Will I curse God or bless his name even if my teeth are clenched in agony as I worship? Will I let the presence and power of God fill me to overflowing when I have nothing left to give, or will I seek to make it through in my own strength?

Powerful people seek to face suffering by relying on their own reserve of strength and tenacity.

The powerless throw in the towel as soon as the winds shift, long before the roof comes crashing down.

But the *empowered* hold the hand of Jesus and let his strength and presence carry them through the tempest of suffering, loss, and pain. The empowered know that they can't weather the storms life will bring, but that the Maker of heaven and earth can place them under his wings and shelter them no matter what comes their way.

When relentless suffering and pain show up on your doorstep—and they will show up—cling to Jesus. Don't be confident in your own strength and power. Don't feel powerless and victimized. Draw from the source of all power. Cling to the One who gave his life to save you, love you, and redeem you from the pit.

When your arms grow limp, your hands are cramped and can cling no longer, feel the arms of Jesus wrap around you and be certain that he will never let you go. You will be empowered by the presence and strength of the Savior, the One through whom the heavens and earth came to be. As he holds you, whisper these words through chapped, bruised, or bloodied lips:

> Naked I came from my mother's womb,
>   and naked I will depart.
> The LORD gave and the LORD has taken away;
>   may the name of the LORD be praised. (Job 1:21)

From the Heart of Job

Dear Friend,

Hold on to God. Even when the storms come, the roof crashes down, and your loss feels so deep and painful that you are certain you can't make it through another day.

God is still on the throne. He really is. He made the heavens and the earth. He is powerful and sovereign. He loves you and has a good plan for your life. Your story is still being written and God is the author.

God gives, and he takes away, but his name is always worthy of praise and blessing.

Though your body is ravaged, your heart is broken, your finances evaporated, and your friends seem useless in your pain, God is still God. Hold on to him in faith. Be relentless in trust. Open your eyes and see the One who rules, reigns, and loves you, even when you look to him through a river of tears. He is still God. He is near. He has not forgotten you.

▸▸ **Walk with Job** and learn more of his journey of being empowered through suffering by reading Job 1–7 and Job 38–42.

2

Paul's 195 Scars

Facing Abuse for Doing the Right Thing

I have worked much harder, been in prison more frequently, been flogged more severely, and been exposed to death again and again. Five times I received from the Jews the forty lashes minus one. Three times I was beaten with rods, once I was pelted with stones, three times I was shipwrecked, I spent a night and a day in the open sea.

2 Corinthians 11:23–25

Three times I pleaded with the Lord to take it away from me. But he said to me, "My grace is sufficient for you, for my power is made perfect in weakness." Therefore I will boast all the more gladly about my weaknesses, so that Christ's power may rest on me. That is why, for Christ's sake, I delight in weaknesses, in insults, in hardships, in persecutions, in difficulties. For when I am weak, then I am strong.

2 Corinthians 12:8–10

When he woke up that morning, he had no idea what he would see or experience. I guess none of us really does. He was a workingman. He did his job and he did it well. He worked for the government, and disciplining "troublemakers" was one of the items on his job description. With years of practice, he had mastered his trade.

When a person broke the law, was accused of wrongdoing, or caused trouble, he meted out the punishment designated by the religious or political establishment. One of those punishments was aptly called "the forty lashes less one." The Jewish Law forbade lashing anyone more than forty times. So, in an effort to make sure they never crossed this line, they took one step back and would only lash a person thirty-nine times. This gave a little buffer to make sure no one lost count, crossed the threshold of forty, and broke the Law while they were seeking to uphold it.

When the Jewish leaders brought charges or accusations, his job was simple. He would strap the man up, hands above his head, tear off his robe in a very public setting, and bring the whip down on his back, chest, and sides thirty-nine times. He was fairly hardened to the pain people suffered . . . that's what happens when part of your job description is beating people within an inch of their life. Tender hearts don't last long in that line of work. He could handle almost anything, or so he thought.

When he strapped up the Christian troublemaker named Paul, he was not ready for what he saw. This teacher did not seem criminal. He was more of an academic than a lawbreaker. He was a preacher. He was kind to the guards and other enforcers of the law. This man everyone called "the Apostle Paul" actually exuded grace, not anger and hatred.

All he knew was that he had a job to do and today his checklist included giving this gentle man the forty lashes less one. When he tore off Paul's robes, he stood in stunned amazement. As he surveyed Paul's naked upper body, he could not find a single piece of flesh that was not covered with scars. This Christian preacher was a human tapestry of mutilated flesh. He realized that Paul had received the thirty-nine lashes a number of times already. What he did not know was this would be the fifth time Paul was strapped up, stripped down, and scourged. Paul already had 156 scars embedded on his body and soul.

There was no fresh flesh left, no place to strike where Paul had not felt the searing and tearing pain of the whip on his body. So, the man did his job. He added scars upon scars. With the first strike, Paul received the 157th blow, and when he was done, Paul felt, through mind-numbing and blinding pain, the last of 195 lashes.

195 scars. 195 blows. 195 times Paul felt the scourge fall on his body.

What goes through your mind when you are being strapped up for the fifth time, knowing exactly what is going to happen next? What do you think as they strip your tunic off and expose what is left of your flesh to the world and the whip? What do you pray to the God you love, the Jesus you follow, the Spirit of comfort you have written about so many times, as you brace yourself for the scorpion sting of the scourge thirty-nine more times?

We must remember that this man being beaten for the fifth time was being punished for nothing other than living for Jesus and following the will of God.

Sometime in the past, Paul had been passionately preaching about Jesus, and the consequence for sharing the love of the Savior was the unique and public torture of scourging—the forty lashes less one. When they were finished, the apostle Paul had thirty-nine tears in his flesh that would become thirty-nine scars. What did he do? Quit preaching? Stop following Jesus? Back off or tone down his Christ-centered rhetoric? No, he kept preaching, following, and standing for the Savior he loved.

In response, they scourged Paul a second time. His resolve did not weaken. His faith grew stronger. With seventy-eight stripes on his body, he was emboldened and empowered to press on.

Later, after another fabricated provocation, they beat him again. One hundred seventeen scars marked the body of the preacher of grace. Now maybe he would back off, or at least tone down his bold declarations about Jesus being God, Savior, the only way to the Father.

He did no such thing. They could not beat the power of God or the good news of the gospel out of this man. So they bound his arms, ripped off his clothing, and scourged him again. Surely this would break the man. If he had any sense, he would shut his mouth and drop the whole "Jesus is Savior" declaration. Would 156 lashes be enough to silence him? Would he finally stop declaring that Jesus alone could bear our sins and offer us forgiveness? No! Love still poured from his lips, grace from his pen as he wrote to the churches, and he continued to declare the lifesaving message of Jesus.

This led to the fifth time Paul would receive the forty lashes minus one. When the soldier finished and dealt the final blow, Paul had 195 scars on his body. Scars on scars on scars.

What is shocking is that Paul's body bore even more signs of his relentless faithfulness to Jesus. Three times he was beaten with rods . . . what kind of mark does that leave? Once he was stoned and left for dead. In his second letter to the Corinthian church, Paul gives a list of the many and varied ways that people tried to silence him, break his spirit, and stop him from telling the world about Jesus.

How do you find strength to press on and keep sharing the gospel after all this suffering? The truth is, none of us can do this in our own power. We can't muster up the strength. Positive attitude is not enough. This kind of faithful following in the face of brutal persecution can only come when we are empowered. When God's strength is made perfect in our weakness.

Powerful people proclaim, "I will take anything for Jesus." But in our own power, facing thirty-nine lashes would mute and stop even the most powerful of us.

The powerless run for the hills, shut their mouth, and stop talking about Jesus at the threat of judgment, punishment, or discipline . . . before the first blow falls.

Empowered people know they don't have strength to stand up against persecution and hardship, but the moment-by-moment presence and filling of the Holy Spirit carries them through. They stand strong, even if their legs are trembling.

Paul did not keep preaching because he was powerful. He did not run away because he felt powerless. Paul was empowered by the Holy Spirit, just as Jesus had promised before he ascended into heaven:

> But you will receive power when the Holy Spirit comes on you; and you will be my witnesses.[1]

So, with scars upon scars, Paul got up and preached again. He did this knowing that it could cost him another scourging and another thirty-nine scars, or even his life.

From the Heart of Paul

Dear Brothers and Sisters,

You feel beat down, discouraged, and disheartened. You have sought, with a pure heart, to follow Jesus, but things have not turned out like you anticipated. You wonder, does God care, is he watching over me, can I press on and keep standing for Jesus under the weight of my pain?

The answer is yes, yes, and yes! God cares beyond your comprehension. He sees you and is with you. And, God is ready to empower you for the next step of your journey.

The closer you walk with Jesus, the more you will learn that faithful servants do not stroll through life unscathed and march into heaven unscarred. We who walk closely with the crucified One will stumble forward, bearing the scars of being a disciple. We will hobble onward empowered by the Holy Spirit for one more day, one more battle, one more step of faithful following. Then, if we have to, we will crawl across the finish line with our lives poured out as a sacrifice for the Savior who bore the nails, the scourge, the mocking, and our sins.

On that day you will fall into the arms of your faithful Lord and feel his nail-pierced hands embrace you. You will hear him say, "Well done, good and faithful servant," and you will be home.

▸▸ **Walk with Paul** and learn more of his journey of being empowered through times of suffering by reading Acts 13–28; 2 Corinthians 11:16–33 and 12:8–10.

3

Hannah's Sorrow and Tears

When Dreams Don't Come True

"Not so, my lord," Hannah replied, "I am a woman who is deeply troubled. I have not been drinking wine or beer; I was pouring out my soul to the LORD. Do not take your servant for a wicked woman; I have been praying here out of my great anguish and grief."

1 Samuel 1:15–16

We live in a Disneyland culture. Many young girls have grown up on a steady diet of animated "Princess" movies made by Disney. From the classics like Cinderella and Snow White to more modern princesses like Ariel, Belle, and Pocahontas, these cartoon characters affirm the Disney theme song, "When you wish upon a star your dreams come true." This tune opened the movie *Pinocchio* and ended up winning an Academy Award for best original song. There seems to be a recurring theme in Disney lore that puppets can become real boys, ordinary girls can become princesses, and dreams come true if we can just find the right star to wish upon!

The problem is, Disney theology and biblical theology are dramatically different. The characters we meet on the pages of

Scripture are not animated and illustrated but flesh and blood human beings. Things don't always go their way. Dreams don't always come true. And suffering is often a core part of their story and journey.

Such was the case for Hannah.

One word marked her life. It defined her. Such was the way of the ancient world in which Hannah lived. The word was *barren*.

We won't get into all the cultural details, but in those days, many men had more than one wife and this was the case in the household of Elkanah. Jewish tradition teaches that Elkanah had two wives. Hannah was the first and his beloved. But after ten years of barrenness, in order to fulfill the biblical call to "be fruitful and multiply," he took a second wife named Peninnah so that he could have children and carry on the family name. The midrash (ancient rabbinical teachings) filled in the blanks and posits that Peninnah had ten sons.[1]

Not only did Peninnah excel in bearing children for her husband, Elkanah, but she was a master at imposing emotional torment. Hannah's dreams were not coming true and Peninnah rubbed her nose in it every chance she could.[2]

How long does it take to bear ten sons? Add this to the ten years Hannah suffered before Peninnah entered the picture. It seems that over two decades had passed while Hannah "wept," "agonized," "anguished," and "grieved." These are the words the Bible uses to paint a picture of this woman.

This was no Disney tale of wishing upon a star, waking up the next day, and finding Prince Charming at her side. This is no conflict and resolution that would be wrapped up with a "happily ever after" in ninety minutes with a catchy tune to play while the credits rolled. Hannah was a real woman, with real tears, facing deep loss . . . year after year after painful year.

Finally, more than twenty years into her marriage and journey of infertility, Hannah suffered one more insult. She joined her husband on his yearly pilgrimage to the place of worship in Shiloh. Because her rival Peninnah openly provoked and taunted her, Hannah wept and could not eat. She went to the place of worship and cried out to God in prayer from deep parts of herself that were beyond words. Again and again she groaned her prayers to God from her emotional pit of despair.

Her passionate pleas and cries to Yahweh were interrupted by the voice of the great priest Eli. His words were not affirming. They were not kind. They were not sensitive. He accused her of being drunk! He told her to stop hitting the bottle so early in the day.

She had to explain to the town pastor that she was not drunk but crying out to God from deep in her soul. She let him know that she was not wicked and running away from God and to a bottle. Instead, she was running to God in the midst of her anguish and grief.

Just think about it. More than twenty years of pain. Two hundred forty monthly cycles of hoping for pregnancy and facing the reality that it would not be this month. Yet Hannah did not quit praying. She did not give up on God. She was broken, hurting, afflicted, but still trusting. Twenty spring seasons watching everything blossom around her and nothing bloom within her. Hannah's dreams remained exactly that—dreams.

As she encountered the prophet Eli and defended her character, he extended a word of blessing and a prayer: "Go in peace, and may the God of Israel grant you what you have asked of him."[3] Could she hope? Would she dare believe that her womb would be opened and she might bear a child? And what of her prayer, her promise, her commitment to God?

A year later Hannah held a baby in her arms.

This was not another child of Peninnah or even the baby of a neighbor who asked Hannah to help out and watch her little one for an afternoon. This was Samuel, Hannah's own son. This was the boy who would become one of the greatest leaders in the history of God's people. This was the fulfillment of her dreams, but it would not be a Disney ending.

You see, Hannah had made a promise to God. "Lord, if you give me a son, I will surrender him to your service all the days of his life."[4] She had committed to give her firstborn son to the service of the priesthood. This would mean weaning him and handing him over to the priest Eli. The same man who had first accused her of being drunk and then had spoken a prayer of blessing over her. It would mean traveling to Shiloh with her child at her side and turning around to go home alone. This was not the "happily ever after" ending most women dream about.

This was Hannah's story. Once a year she would make a robe for her son, the boy-minister-in-training. She would take an annual journey with her husband to Shiloh and visit her boy, Samuel. That would be the extent of their relationship and contact.

A little boy grows a lot in 365 days. She watched her son travel through childhood to adolescence and into manhood in once-a-year snapshots. "My, how you have grown," "You are looking more and more like your father every year," "You have facial hair . . . when did you become a man?" Hannah would visit, deliver a new robe, gaze on her boy as only a mother can, pour out her heart to her son, and then trek home. Her anticipation of seeing him again in a year would begin while she was still on the way back from this year's trip to Shiloh.

How do you stay empowered when the clock ticks and life seems to be slipping away? How do you stay filled up when your heart feels like a broken vessel that leaks quicker than you can replenish it? You cling to God in the dark nights of tears and agony. You believe in the One who has oceans of grace at his disposal. You grow the roots of your faith deep in the One who is immovable and immutable.

Powerful people work with all their might to make their dreams a reality. If they accomplish what they set out to do, they can pat themselves on the back and celebrate their ability to buck the odds and write their own fairy-tale ending.

The powerless don't dare to dream. They know that Disneyland is a theme park and they have decided that real life is about shattered dreams and lost hope.

Empowered people let God write the script and hold on no matter what twists and turns come on the roller coaster of life. They peek behind the veil and discover that God has dreams for his children, but they rarely follow the formula of an animated princess tale.

The timetable is not often what we would decide or choose. There might be more tears along the path than we would script. But at the end of the story, God is glorified and we have become more like him. Hannah's road was not easy, but she followed the Lord through years of heartache. Today she stands as an example of resilient faith. Her version of "happily ever after" might not have materialized, but God's dreams were born of her womb and the ancient world was changed through a prophet named Samuel, the son of Hannah.

From the Heart of Hannah

My Friend,

You are waiting, longing, praying, and dreaming. You wonder when everything will be made right and make sense. You still imagine that all your dreams might come true and your ending will be like ancient and modern fairy tales.

God is bigger than our dreams. Were he not, our meager imaginations would limit the wonder any of us could ever experience. God's plans encompass more than our personal wants and desires. He rules the universe and actually knows what he is doing. He really does!

Trust God, even when it seems your prayers are not being answered. Even when you have choked out the same prayer for twenty years. Keep trusting.

Even when the script of your life does not make sense to you. When you look over your shoulder and see your dreams fade on the horizon, hold on. Trust God because he is worthy. One day, in this life or the next, you will look back and see that God bore something in and through you that accomplished his dream, his plan, and brought him glory.

When God's dreams become yours, you will learn that the life of every faithful believer is exactly what God designed it to be. From the vantage point of heaven, your life will end with the words, "Happily ever after."

▸▸ **Walk with Hannah** and learn more of her journey of being empowered through waiting, sorrow, and disappointment by reading 1 Samuel 1:1–2:11.

4

Joseph's Journey of Loss

Far from Home But Close to God

Now Joseph had been taken down to Egypt. Potiphar, an Egyptian who was one of Pharaoh's officials, the captain of the guard, bought him from the Ishmaelites who had taken him there. The LORD was with Joseph so that he prospered, and he lived in the house of his Egyptian master.

Genesis 39:1–2

But while Joseph was there in the prison, the LORD was with him; he showed him kindness and granted him favor in the eyes of the prison warden.

Genesis 39:20–21

The year was 1841 and Solomon's life was hard but good. He had a gracious wife, three beautiful children, and a cozy home. He juggled two jobs to make ends meet. By day he worked as a skilled carpenter, and at night and on weekends he leveraged his skills on the violin for extra income. His musical talents were in demand

39

in New York, where he lived, but he also traveled to Canada and other places to play the fiddle and entertain enthusiastic listeners.

It would seem his life was quite ordinary for that time and place in history, except that Solomon was a black man in pre–Civil War America. He was free but aware that slavery plagued the South and many other parts of the world. Solomon Northup had some idea of the cruelty of slavery, but had never felt the cold of iron shackles against his skin or the searing pain of a whip on his back.

All of that was about to change.

Solomon was offered two weeks of work and excellent pay to travel and play his violin. The men who hired him had other intentions in mind. They sold him to slavers who accused him of being a runaway from Georgia. What followed was twelve years of torment, pain, abuse, and separation that Solomon could have never imagined before he experienced them.

He was beaten repeatedly by a heartless slave trader who intended to break him and sell him. His first "master," William Ford, showed a measure of kindness, and as Solomon served him well, he actually gave him a violin as a gift. When Solomon tried to tell Ford that he was not actually a runaway slave but a free man, Ford did not want to hear the truth. He was more concerned with his own financial investment in Solomon. Solomon soon faced conflict with a cruel and power-hungry man who worked for Ford and with time he was sold again.

The glimmer of hope and kindness he saw in the eyes of William Ford was nowhere to be seen in the hate-filled glare of his second master. Edwin Epps was heartless and heavy handed. He believed it was his God-given right to own and beat slaves, and he saw them as less than human. Any of his slaves who did not pick two hundred pounds of cotton a day were severely beaten. Solomon was often short on this cotton quota and his back became evidence of his master's severity.

When Epps was forced to "lease" his slaves out to another plantation owner due to a lack of work on his cotton farm, Solomon once again saw a ray of hope and a chance to acquire his freedom. He asked a white farmhand, who seemed kind and fair, if he would secretly mail a letter to his friends in New York so they could rescue him. This man turned on Solomon, took his money, and reported his effort to "escape" to the plantation owner. Solomon's trust was again shattered and his hope dashed.

When more than a decade had passed, Solomon had learned to act the part of a slave. He was broken, but not entirely hopeless. He was back working on the farm of Epps, his second master, and was again being beaten when his quota of cotton fell below the prescribed weight. He was assigned to work on a carpentry project with a white man who freely and publicly spoke to Epps of his opposition to the institution of slavery. Solomon wondered if he dared to ask this man for help. In desperation, Solomon confided in one more person and told him he was actually a free man, a husband, and the father of three children he had not seen for almost a dozen years. He begged for help and he received it!

After twelve years of brutal slavery and separation from his family, Solomon Northup was freed and returned to his home and family. He was one of the few free black men or women at that time in history who were sold into slavery but finally regained their freedom and were able to tell their story. His story became an award-winning movie based on the book *Twelve Years a Slave*, written by Solomon Northup himself.[1]

About 1900 BC another story of a free man being sold into slavery played out. Favored by his father, hated by his brothers, thrown in a pit, sold as a slave, unjustly imprisoned, forgotten by those he helped, and feared by those he loved. These are some of the cliffs notes from the life of Joseph. He begged his brothers to have mercy on him, but his pleas fell on deaf ears and rock-hard hearts. Joseph was bound with ropes and bound for a whole new life.

As the Midianite traders started south toward Egypt, Joseph's dreams grew smaller and smaller as his brothers and homeland disappeared over the horizon. In this strange new world, Joseph would be sold again, like a piece of meat in a market. A slave, forgotten and abandoned.

He began as a loved and favored child, he had dreams from God, and he seemed destined for greatness. In what seemed like the snap of a finger, young Joseph became a stranger in a strange land. He was a slave under the thumb of a politician named Potiphar.

What would happen to Joseph's faith in Yahweh, the God of Israel, when he was abandoned by family, sold as a slave, and made to live and work among a people he did not know? How would Joseph survive in a land where he did not understand the language and customs of the people? In Joseph's day, many cultures believed that their god was powerful and influential within their nation's territorial boundaries but impotent beyond their borders. The thinking at that time was that the gods of Egypt, and there were many of them, had power in that country and other nations' gods had no influence there. It would have been easy for Joseph to abandon Yahweh when he crossed into Egypt. To all outward appearances, Yahweh had abandoned him. Why remain faithful?

Joseph did not switch gods at the border. He did not buy into the thinking of the day and assume that his God was powerless in another country. Instead, Joseph's resolve grew stronger. He did not deny his faith but drove the tent stakes of his heart deep into the soil of his love for Yahweh, even in a foreign land. What we read over and over again in Joseph's story is that "the LORD was with Joseph." Again and again we see this young man stay faithful to God even when he was far from his home and his suffering seemed to keep escalating.

When the wife of his master Potiphar made sexual advances on Joseph, he did not rationalize potential sin or justify a "youthful indiscretion" because he was far from home. He did not taste of the forbidden fruit and say to himself, "What happens in Egypt stays in Egypt." Instead, he refused her advances and held his ground. Joseph maintained his integrity far from home.

What was the result of his faithfulness and devotion to God? Potiphar's wife lied about him, made false accusations, flipped the tables, and Joseph was thrown into the deep dark dungeon of Pharaoh. Have you ever been in a dungeon? Locked up. Hopeless. Abandoned. Unjustly condemned. Alone.

Even in a foreign land and consigned to a dungeon, we read that "the LORD was with him; he showed him kindness."[2] Where do we meet God and experience his empowering presence? On the mountaintop when things are going wonderfully? Yes! But also in the depths of despair and life's dungeons.

If we could have watched Joseph's life and followed him through his dizzying spiral downward from favored son in his homeland to imprisoned "criminal" in a foreign country, we might expect him to throw in the towel and give up on God. We might wonder if the accusations of Potiphar's licentious wife would break Joseph and finally dash his faith to pieces. When he argued his innocence and was incarcerated anyway, this might have been the time in Joseph's journey where he would finally reject his faith and take an easier route. Somehow Joseph received power to stand strong. He was empowered to hold fast, press on, and cling to the hand of the God who was still with him, even when every outside sign flashed these neon words: "YOU ARE ALONE!"

You would think that things could not get any worse, but they did. Sometime later, still in prison, Joseph interpreted a dream for a leader in Pharaoh's cabinet who had also been tossed into jail. In a short time the dream came true, exactly as Joseph had said. Joseph had made one simple request: "Remember me when you get out of here."[3] When the cupbearer got back to his life of luxury and place of prominence, he immediately forgot the help Joseph had given him and the heartfelt plea Joseph had made. It just slipped his mind . . . for two whole years! Over seven hundred days and nights later, while Joseph was still rotting in the dungeon, Pharaoh had some dreams of his own and needed someone to interpret them. At this point the cupbearer smacked his own forehead and had a "How could I have forgotten" moment. He remembered Joseph and called him to stand before the king and help make sense of his dreams.

At this point, for the first time since Joseph was thrown in a pit by his brothers, things took a turn for the better! The best estimate is that thirteen years had passed from the time Joseph was sold as a slave to the Egyptians until he was finally set free from his bondage in Pharaoh's dungeon. Thirteen years of rejection, abandonment, sorrow, abuse, loneliness, slavery, and clinging to faith in the darkness. Yet, through it all, "the LORD was with Joseph"[4] and Joseph held on to God.

Both Solomon Northup and Joseph were sold into slavery. Solomon by strangers, Joseph by his own brothers. Both men were cut off from their loved ones, sent from home, abused greatly, and finally, set free. When Solomon was back in New York, he did what most normal people would do. He devoted a great deal of time to seeking justice and the punishment of those who had wronged him. Joseph's response was quite different, shocking, and unusual. When he finally faced the very ones who sold him off as a slave, he extended grace, compassion, and he cared for them.[5]

Powerful people shake a defiant fist in the face of oppression and dig their heels deep into the soil of their own sense of indignation. When the world rages against them, they rage back.

Powerless people toss God aside when he does not perform up to their expectations. Once they cross the border of life's pain, they cling to the next god that presents itself and seems sufficient for their needs.

When an *empowered* follower of God sees dreams shattered, feels forgotten by loved ones, and has life turn against them, they hold on to the one true source of power. An empowered life of faith is fueled by an unyielding confidence that God is still with us, even when every outside sign says we are alone. There is no place we can go that is outside the bounds of God's sovereign strength and grace.

Like Joseph we must learn to cling to the One who is still with us even when we are thrown in a pit, abandoned by family, stripped of human kindness, unjustly locked up, lied about, and forgotten by those we have helped and served. No matter how far away we wander or are taken, we find our home and strength in the God who is with us always.

From the Heart of Joseph

Dear Friend,

Have you been abandoned by family, betrayed by those you have helped, thrown in life's pit, or forgotten in a prison of pain? Does it feel like God has deserted you and left you adrift on the sea to be blown by the fickle winds of fate? Are you about ready to give up on God, faith, and the promises of the Scriptures?

Don't! Please, don't give up!

God is still with you. He has an amazing plan and you are part of it. Hang in there and don't cave to the countless temptations that cry out for your attention. Being alone in Egypt offers many enticements but none of them are worth your soul. Turn and run. Run from sin and directly into the arms of God.

As dark as things look and as dank as the dungeon might be, you are not alone. God is with you. He is accomplishing his plan in and through you. You might not see the light at the end of your tunnel, but the light of God is in your heart and sometimes that has to be enough.

▶▶ **Walk with Joseph** and learn more of his journey of being empowered through a long season of rejection and pain by reading Genesis 37–50.

5

Peter, a Disciple's Sacrifice

Trading Everything for Jesus

As Jesus was walking beside the Sea of Galilee, he saw two brothers, Simon called Peter and his brother Andrew. They were casting a net into the lake, for they were fishermen. "Come, follow me," Jesus said, "and I will send you out to fish for people." At once they left their nets and followed him.

Matthew 4:18–20

Some of life's suffering and loss comes unannounced and unexpected. Like a car running a red light and blindsiding us, our life is altered in a split second. We simply don't see it coming, but the impact is undeniable.

At other times, the pain of life comes to the front door, knocks, and says, "May I come in and stay with you?" There are actually times we make conscious choices we know will lead to inevitable suffering and pain. We invite it in. On the road of life we are assured that certain choices come with a cost attached, yet we willingly open the door and embrace the consequences because it is the right thing to do.

Having kids is like this. From the discomfort of pregnancy, to the pain of delivery, to facing heartaches through the years, it is not easy being a parent. But it is worth the cost.

My wife, Sherry, and I got married almost three decades ago. We have raised three sons who are all adults, out of the house, and each one is walking in a growing relationship with Jesus. But it was not always easy! We faced many of the same challenges other parents have faced as we raised our boys. We spent plenty of time on our knees in prayer. We shed our fair share of tears along the way.

If we had known all the challenges and heartaches that come with parenting, we might not have signed up for the duty. If someone wrote a book that outlined *every* sacrifice and *every* price that must be paid to raise children well, I wonder if anyone would rise to the task. The truth is, no one who becomes a mom or dad enters in with full awareness of what they are doing, and that might just be good.

When Jesus called people to follow, he did not candy-coat what it would mean to be his disciple. He was honest, blunt, and crystal clear. Try this on for size:

> Then he said to them all: "Whoever wants to be my disciple must deny themselves and take up their cross daily and follow me. For whoever wants to save their life will lose it, but whoever loses their life for me will save it. What good is it for someone to gain the whole world, and yet lose or forfeit their very self?" (Luke 9:23–25)

What piercing invitations:

Deny yourself.
Take up your cross.
Follow Jesus.
Lose your life.

Most of us unconsciously soften a passage like this by thinking of these words as spiritual images to remind us that becoming a Christian might have a few inconvenient bumps along the road, but we tell ourselves it will all be worth it when we pull into the driveway of our heavenly mansion.

What if we are wrong? What if this call of Jesus is far more literal, rigorous, and reckless than we realize?[1] It certainly was for the first disciples. When they said yes to his call, they traded everything and put their whole life on the line for the sake of knowing and living for Jesus.

Peter left his family and vocation to become a Christ-follower. He was in the middle of a workday, casting nets into the Sea of Galilee with his partner in the family fishing business when Jesus said, "Come, follow me."[2] From that moment on, Peter's life was radically altered. He left his family, his home, the security of his job, and almost everything he knew so he could follow this rabbi named Jesus.

Along the way, Peter endured intense hardship, faced persecution, and suffered much as he followed the Savior. Denying himself took on real and tangible meaning as his dreams and plans were set aside and the will and ministry of Jesus became his consuming passion. At one point Peter actually spoke up and said to Jesus, "We have left everything to follow you!"[3] He felt the cost of denying himself day after day. It was a conscious choice.

Jesus warned his disciples, before they signed on, that following him would mean taking up their cross and losing their life. Today people use this line in a very different way. We hear statements like, "My neighbor is really hard to get along with and they are extremely irritating, but that's the cross I bear." Or, "I am lactose intolerant. It is really a hassle, but that's the cross I bear." Somehow our minor inconveniences and annoyances are categorized as "bearing a cross." This kind of thinking radically misses the point.

Peter followed Jesus with absolute commitment to the end of his life. Church history tells us that it led him to an actual cross. When the Roman emperor Nero Augustus Caesar was persecuting Christians, he brought his insane fury down on church leaders, and Peter was one of them. Around AD 67–68 Peter, "the Rock," was martyred by crucifixion. The early church father Origen records that when Peter was told he would be crucified, he asked that it would be upside down because he was not deserving a death like that of Jesus. His executioners accommodated his request and Peter gave up his life rather than renounce his faith in Jesus and devotion to the Savior.[4]

What did Peter give up, sacrifice, and trade when he decided to follow Jesus? The answer is clear—everything! He surrendered his very life.

What does this mean for you and me? How do we follow in the steps of the Lord and walk as his disciples in this world? We are called to deny ourselves, take up the cross of Jesus, and follow him wherever he leads.

This will look different for each of us, but the call to total and absolute surrender is the same. Set down your goals and dreams and follow the call of Jesus. Watch where the Savior is going and walk in his footsteps. Go where he calls you to go, love who he calls you to love, forgive who he calls you to forgive, serve who he calls you to serve, give what he calls you to give, and sacrifice what he calls you to sacrifice. Take up your cross every day. Be willing to lay your life down for Jesus. The cross is *not* primarily a decoration, it is *not* a metaphor, and it is *not* a picture of life's minor nuisances. The cross was a place where people were brutally executed. It was a picture of death. It still is.

Have you ever wondered why most Christians today don't seem to suffer much for their faith? It might be because we have stopped opening our mouths and talking about Jesus and the biblical faith we claim to believe. We are often afraid to offend, ruffle feathers, or make waves.

What repercussions might we face if we opened our mouths and called people to justice when injustice seems to be ruling the day? What might happen if we spoke up for biblical morality in a world that demands tolerance of any and every lifestyle choice no matter how immoral? How might people respond if we humbly, yet confidently, explained that we believe that every person on this planet really does need Jesus? How would our friends, family members, and colleagues react if we held to biblical truth even when it seems antiquated and outdated?

Following Jesus and counting the cost are more than simply saying we love the Savior. To take up the cross is to lay down our lives. This is the call of a disciple. This includes speaking up, acting out, taking chances, and even suffering for the cause and name of Jesus. Each day is a new chance to trade everything for the One who gave his life for us on the hill called Calvary.

The powerful hear the call of Jesus and say, "I can do this." They seek to sacrifice, serve, and follow in their own strength. They have no idea how far Jesus might take them from home and what he might call them to do.

The powerless hear the call to follow Jesus, lay down their life, their dreams, and their plans for the future, but they resist. They cling to the security of their nets and boats. They keep their mouth shut and their head down.

Empowered people learn, very quickly, that their abilities and personal potency will not give them what they need to deny self, take up the cross, and follow in the footsteps of Jesus. But they are ready and willing to follow.

With trembling heart and deep prayers for the filling of the Holy Spirit, they drop their nets, leave the security of the past, and they walk forward. As they follow Jesus they learn that suffering, loss, and pain are part of the journey. They live a countercultural life when God calls them to do so. They open their mouth and speak up for Jesus, even when the world mocks, resists, and abuses. They know that walking next to Jesus always means experiencing collateral damage, because the full artillery of hell and earthly forces of evil are unleashed against Jesus and his followers.

Peter dropped his nets, left his family, and followed the Savior. His journey started on the shore of the Sea of Galilee and ended on a Roman cross with his feet pointing toward heaven. But this was not the end of Peter's story. When he breathed his last gasp of air on this earth, he was swept into the strong arms of the One for whom Peter had traded it all.

The trade was worth it.

From the Heart of Peter

Fellow Disciple,

What does it look like when a person hears the call of Jesus to deny self, take up the cross, and follow? It is a call to die. Every day if need be. We are to live for Jesus with such complete surrender and passion that we are ready to give all of our life. If, one day, this means dying for Jesus, we should have already made the decision and be willing to give the ultimate sacrifice for the One who gave his life for us.

Drop your nets and leave your boat. Don't cling to the false security this world promises. Just follow Jesus.

Love your family, but never more than you love the Savior. Keep Jesus, his mission, and his vision in the center of your heart.

In the times of sacrifice, struggle, and suffering, hold on to the One who is holding on to you. His power will be enough. He will fill you. He will carry you through. And when this life ends, be it sooner or later, he will be right there, ready to bring you home.

▶▶ **Walk with Peter** and learn more of his journey of being empowered by sacrificing everything for Jesus as you read Matthew 4:18–20; 10:1–20; 14:22–36; 16:13–17:13; 18:21–35; 26:31–35, 69–75; John 21.

Jesus's Scream of Loneliness

Our Example of Suffering
with Purpose

From noon until three in the afternoon darkness came over all the land. About three in the afternoon Jesus cried out in a loud voice, "Eli, Eli, lema sabachthani?" (which means "My God, my God, why have you forsaken me?").

Matthew 27:45–46

What does Jesus say when the nails pierce his hands and feet, when crowds mock, when friends have run for the hills, and when the sins of all human beings are being poured out on him? What cry comes from the mouth of God's beautiful and spotless Lamb when he is taking away the sins of the world? What question comes from the mouth of the sin-crushed Savior as the wrath of his Father is poured out on the one and only Son of God?

Eli, Eli, lema sabachthani?

This cry of agony cascaded from the cross and down the hill called Golgotha. The question must be heard today, over two thousand years later. This question still resounds and echoes through the hearts of every follower of Jesus. It will never go away. It never should.

Eli, Eli, lema sabachthani?

The declaration and question go hand in hand. "My God, my God, why have you forsaken me?" No one in the history of the world has suffered as much as Jesus. There is no other example that could possibly surpass Jesus's example of grace and strength in the midst of crushing pain and agony.

So often when we speak of the cross of Jesus and think about his sacrificial death for our sins, we fixate on the physical pain he endured. This is right and as it should be. Jesus endured the exact physical pain that we would have endured had we taken the nails, the crown of thorns, and the scourging.

Years ago, when I was a youth pastor, a seventh-grade girl came up to me and said, "I think I know what Jesus did when he was on the cross!" I was not sure what she was getting at. She was a new believer and had talked to me about how hard it was to think of Jesus suffering and enduring the pain of the cross for "her sins." It bothered her. She could not let it go.

In response to the struggle with the theological reality of the agony Jesus had endured, this young girl had really gone to work on reconciling her emotional pain with the physical suffering of Jesus. She had come up with a solution that would help her live with the discomfort of imagining Jesus's experience of the nails piercing his hands and feet and the scourge falling on his back.

She looked at me and explained, "Jesus was God, right?" I affirmed that indeed he is fully divine. "Then I think he made it so he would not feel the pain. He had the power to do that." I could see that this "theory" brought her relief and comfort. The problem is, she was wrong. Her tender heart had fashioned a theological perspective that made her feel better, but it was inaccurate.

I looked into her hopeful eyes and said, "Can I tell you the truth about what Jesus did on the cross?" She nodded her head slowly in the affirmative. I gently explained, "I know this is hard to hear, but Jesus felt all the pain of the crucifixion. He died in your place and mine, for our sins. He took our punishment. The judgment we deserved was placed on him." I swallowed and said, "Jesus felt exactly what you would have felt if you had been nailed to the cross. This is the only way he could pay the price for your sins and be your substitute."

Tears welled up in her junior high eyes and began to stream down her face. As hard as it was for her to hear this truth, I knew she needed to know exactly what Jesus had done for her. We all do.

Jesus bore the physical pain of the cross and felt it all. But the suffering did not end there. He bore emotional pain on his road to Calvary. One of his closest followers betrayed him and sold him out for thirty pieces of silver. In the pressure of the arrest of Jesus, all of the disciples fled. Three times Peter, the Rock, denied that he knew Jesus. Peter's words ended in a crescendo of renunciation: "I don't know the man! May I be cursed if I even know him!"[1] At this very moment Jesus locked eyes with his friend Peter.[2] When Peter denied that he knew Jesus, they were both in the same courtyard and the Savior heard it all. On top of all this, the crowds turned on Jesus and their cries of "Hosanna" were exchanged for the declaration, "Crucify!"[3]

Yes, the physical suffering was beyond description. The emotional betrayal and pain were massive and crushing. But, it was the spiritual agony that pierced the heart of the Savior and drove him to scream in a loud voice:

Eli, Eli, lema sabachthani? . . . My God, my God, why have you forsaken me?

The physical and emotional torments were dwarfed by the torture of the spiritual agony Jesus suffered on the cross. "God made him who had no sin to be sin for us, so that in him we might become the righteousness of God."[4] In one incomprehensible moment, all the sins of humanity were placed as a crushing heap of unthinkable evil on the sinless Son of God. The spotless Lamb of heaven was so sin-saturated that he "became sin."

Then the wrath and just judgment of the holy God of heaven fell on Jesus. The punishment we deserved slammed down on our Savior with such spiritual force that no other person could have borne it all. At this moment, something beyond human understanding happened. Jesus, who had always been in perfect communion and harmony with his Father, was alone. In a spiritual sense, as the Father placed our judgment on his beloved Son, Jesus felt the separation we deserved. He was abandoned. Because the Father is holy, holy, holy and can't tolerate sin, he turned his back on the Son. Jesus, who knew no sin, was so consumed by our sin and so under our judgment that he "became sin." At this moment he was utterly and totally alone. His eternal and uninterrupted intimacy with his Father was shattered. He cried out:

Eli, Eli, lema sabachthani? . . . My God, my God, why have you forsaken me?

The good news is that through the suffering and sacrifice of Jesus, we can become the righteousness of God. We can be saved. We can be born again. On the cross of Jesus, the prophecy of Isaiah, given centuries before, became a reality.

> Surely he took up our pain
> and bore our suffering,
> yet we considered him punished by God,
> stricken by him, and afflicted.
> But he was pierced for our transgressions,
> he was crushed for our iniquities;
> the punishment that brought us peace was on him,
> and by his wounds we are healed.
> We all, like sheep, have gone astray,
> each of us has turned to our own way;

and the LORD has laid on him
    the iniquity of us all. (Isa. 53:4–6)

Powerful people seek to work their way to heaven by their own good deeds. They strive, strain, and struggle to pull themselves up by their own spiritual bootstraps. They want to earn their way into the good favor of God. What they don't realize is that the height of God's holiness and the depth of their sin makes it impossible to span the infinite separation, no matter how good they think they are.

Powerless people look at the reality of their own depravity and they know there is no way to earn their way into the presence and favor of a perfect and glorious God. They hang their head in shame and feel unworthy, unloved, and undone. They think, "If there is a way to heaven, I am sure I won't qualify."

Empowered men and women know their efforts will always fall short, but they cast themselves on the amazing grace of Jesus. They are profoundly aware of their depravity but certain of God's power and plan. They look to the cross, draw near to Jesus, and receive the lavish and undeserved grace that was bought with the precious blood of the crucified and risen Savior.

From the Heart of Jesus

Precious One,

Look to the cross. Don't hide your eyes. Don't turn your head, no matter how brutal it is. Open your ears to hear the cry, "My God, my God, why have you forsaken me?"

The price that was paid to cleanse you of sin and win your salvation is greater than you can imagine. It was a gift of love. A willing sacrifice. Heaven's most painful and glorious moment.

At the cross you are healed of all your sin, fears, loneliness, and brokenness. It is hard to comprehend, but a heavenly exchange took place on that hill called Golgotha. At the cross you lay down sin and take up righteousness. You trade your scars for the healing balm of grace. Loneliness dies and you become part of a forever family. Judgment is condemned and heaven is opened. At the cross death dies and new life becomes yours forever.

▸▸ **Walk with Jesus** and learn more of his journey of empowering us through his sacrifice on the cross by reading Matthew 26–27; Mark 14–15; Luke 22–23; and John 18–19.

Resources for Living an Empowered Life

Receiving the Strength You Need Today

Let's be completely honest. No one likes suffering. But, when we look at our past, we discover that the times God does his deepest work in us are often right in the middle of the valleys and during the battles. None of us enjoy hard times and we should not desire struggles to come our way, but these are the very things that can fortify and strengthen us. In moments of pain and loss, God shows up and grows us in ways that could never happen if all of life was smooth sailing.

Here is a sobering reality. Suffering, pain, and loss are sources of strength for a follower of Jesus, and there is no shortage of these things in our world. Just like we can be confident that the sun will rise tomorrow morning, we can know that the pains and hurts of this world will not cease until we see Jesus face-to-face. Until that day, we dare to ask God to use our moments and seasons of suffering, loss, and pain to do something surprising and amazing . . . empower us for the journey ahead.

Here are some ideas, prayers, and activities that can help you plug into God's power through the hard times in life.

Daily Reading Guide for Week 1 of *Empowered*

Use these daily Bible readings and chapters from *Empowered* to gain a solid biblical picture of people who have experienced being empowered through suffering, pain, and loss. Learn and be inspired as you enter into their story.

Day and Character	Daily Bible Reading	Reading from *Empowered*
Day 1—Job	Job 1–2	Chapter 1
Day 2—Paul	Acts 7:54–8:1; 9:1–31; 2 Corinthians 11:16–33; 12:8–10	Chapter 2
Day 3—Hannah	1 Samuel 1:1–2:11	Chapter 3
Day 4—Joseph	Genesis 37; 39–41; 50:15–21	Chapter 4
Day 5—Peter	Matthew 4:18–20; 10:1–20; 14:22–36; 16:13 17:13; 18:21–35; 26:31–35; 26:69–75; John 21	Chapter 5
Weekend—Jesus	Matthew 26–27	Chapter 6

Prayer Guide

Take time to pray using the following prompts and ask God to empower you in fresh new ways:

- Ask God to help you see when you are seeking to be powerful in your own strength and pray for wisdom to stop walking down this dead-end road.

- Invite the Holy Spirit to show you where you are feeling or acting powerless and then to convict you to seek empowerment from God.

- Pray that you will learn to plug into God's many renewable power sources so you can experience being empowered each day.

- Identify a person you care about who has faced painful tragedy and ask God to be near them and to empower them in the coming days.

- Let God know that you are willing to take abuse and face pain for the sake of the gospel, but only pray this if you really mean it.
- Ask for the ability to see how God can bring good out of things that people do with evil intentions.
- Praise God for sending his only Son to pay the price for all your sins.
- Thank Jesus for suffering in your place so that you could be healed, restored to relationship with the Father, and forgiven of all your wrongs.

Journal and Personal Reflections

Write some of your own thoughts and reflections on the following topics and questions:

How have I experienced the empowering presence of God in my life through times of struggle, loss, and pain?

He alone has kept my relationship with my wife together

Who is a person I have watched seek to live in their own power and how have things worked out for them? How can I avoid the dangers of seeking to be powerful in myself?

old friend prior to my conversion (RWJ) He seems bitter + alone

Stay connected by daily devotion, prayer, small groups etc.

What have I learned from watching people who see themselves as powerless and who simply give up and give in? How can I avoid this pitfall?

They lose hope — don't want to see the truth or live in reality — often are in denial.

Where am I trying to be powerful and live in my own abilities or strength?

When I am on auto pilot most of the time, I have to conciously remember to focus on Him.

What are some ways I act or feel like a victim and see myself as powerless? What do the characters in this section of the book teach me about God's power in the lives of ordinary people?

When I feel the sting of rejection or neglect from my wife. or when I feel lonely

— Continue to seek God — never give up hope in God

Write to God and tell him that you are ready and willing (or not too willing but wanting to be) to bear scars if that is the result of following Jesus and sharing his message in this world.

_____

_____

_____

_____

_____

Make a list of some of your personal dreams you are willing to set aside as you yield your whole life to following Jesus.

_____

_____

_____

_____

_____

What are some ways your life has not turned out as you would have planned or imagined? How has God been present through the surprises, twists, and turns in the road?

_____

_____

_____

_____

_____

Action Ideas

Use one or more of the following ideas or exercises to plug into God's power in the coming days:

Study the Sun

Do an internet search on the sun. Discover the immense power and energy available to our planet from this star. Let yourself be amazed at the sheer size of the sun—it is about 864,000 miles wide, and if it were hollow, it could hold more than a million earths!

Then, reflect on the God who made the sun, our earth, you, and everything that exists. The same God who made the sun to warm the earth and maintain life is ready and able to provide all the power you need for anything you will ever face.

Being One of Job's Friends (sort of)

When Job went through his intense time of loss and suffering, some of his friends came to his side to comfort him. There are two dramatically different ways they did this. In the first scene, they simply came with compassion and sat with their friend, feeling with him:

> When Job's three friends, Eliphaz the Temanite, Bildad the Shuhite and Zophar the Naamathite, heard about all the troubles that had come upon him, they set out from their homes and met together by agreement to go and sympathize with him and comfort him. When they saw him from a distance, they could hardly recognize him; they began to weep aloud, and they tore their robes and sprinkled dust on their heads. Then they sat on the ground with him for seven days and seven nights. No one said a word to him, because they saw how great his suffering was. (Job 2:11–13)

In the second scene they debated with him, tried to explain his suffering, placed blame on him, and tormented their friend (Job 4–27).

God wants us to bring compassion and grace to friends in times of loss and pain. He wants to use us as a conduit of his love and care. God is not calling us to beat up on people who are already broken and sorrowing.

Take time in the coming weeks to live out the example of Job's friends in scene one. Identify someone you care about who is really hurting and simply spend time with them. Feel with this person. Pray for them. Bring the presence and grace of Jesus. When you are tempted to move into scene two and try to explain their suffering or figure everything out, quietly say to yourself, "Just keep your mouth shut." This might be the best thing you can do.

Dream Study

Take time to write down some of the dreams you have for your future. Make a list of five dreams you are holding in your heart:

1. _assurance of Salvation for my family_
2. _no more loneliness_
3. _wife to be healed spiritually & physically emotion_
4. _____
5. _____

Next, make a list of at least five dreams you believe God has for your life. These could be attitude shifts, new behaviors of holiness, a step forward in generosity, or some other desire God has for you.

1. _____
2. _____
3. _____
4. _____
5. _____

Finally, take time to prayerfully identify if there are places where your dreams and God's dreams are at odds with each other. If you see an example of this, commit to seek God's dreams above yours, every time!

Where Is God?

For many years people bought books and posters called "Where's Waldo?" The simple idea was to look at complex pictures and find Waldo in his blue jeans, red-and-white-striped shirt, and beanie cap with the red ball on the top. As time passed, many versions of these books appeared in countries all over the world.

In the story of Joseph we discover that God was with this young man in every situation he faced. If we look closely, we can find that God is with us no matter how bad things seem to get. Just like the Waldo books, sometimes we have to look really hard, but when we do, we discover that God was there.

Identify two times in your life when you have faced pain, loss, and suffering. Then reflect closely on how God was with you in these times. Look back, look close, see where God was present, and give him praise.

SECTION 2

Encountering God in the Community of His People

There should be no division in the body, but . . . its parts should have equal concern for each other. If one part suffers, every part suffers with it; if one part is honored, every part rejoices with it.

1 Corinthians 12:25–26

All the believers were one in heart and mind. No one claimed that any of their possessions was their own, but they shared everything they had. With great power the apostles continued to testify to the resurrection of the Lord Jesus. And God's grace was so powerfully at work in them all that there were no needy persons among them. For from time to time those who owned land or houses sold them, brought the money from the sales and put it at the apostles' feet, and it was distributed to anyone who had need.

Acts 4:32–35

7

A Paralytic and His Friends

Are You on the Mat or Carrying It?

Some men came carrying a paralyzed man on a mat and tried to take him into the house to lay him before Jesus. When they could not find a way to do this because of the crowd, they went up on the roof and lowered him on his mat through the tiles into the middle of the crowd, right in front of Jesus.

Luke 5:18–19

Motivated friends. That's what they were.

Jesus was known to be a dynamic teacher, a healer, and a miracle worker. Now he had come to their town, and they were sure that if Jesus could meet their friend, the Lord would certainly restore his legs. The four men literally picked up their friend on his mat and carried him to the place Jesus was teaching.

As had become a standard occurrence, the crowd that gathered to hear Jesus was larger than the venue where the Rabbi was speaking, so people stood at the windows, out the door, and all around the house hoping to hear a few words spoken by Jesus. They were longing to catch a glimpse of the teacher everyone was talking about.

By the time the four men arrived carrying their paralyzed friend, the crowds had beaten them to all the good seats. They could not even get into the house. They had missed their opening . . . or had they?

These highly motivated men did something bold. They crossed the line! In that time of history, and in that part of the world, most homes had a flat roof made of crossbeams covered with branches and packed with mud. There was normally a staircase on the side or back of the house giving access to the roof. These structures were cost-effective, perfect for insulation on hot days, and apparently they were not impenetrable! The four men climbed up and began to dig. They literally made a new entry point to the house above where Jesus was teaching. Once it was big enough, they lowered their friend through the newly designed skylight and into the lap of the teaching Rabbi.

Imagine the picture.

What kind of moxie does it take to destroy a stranger's roof, airlift a friend into a church service, and interrupt Jesus in the middle of a sermon? How motivated do you need to be to circumvent all the norms of the day and deliver a broken friend to the one you know can heal him?

Is there anyone you love enough that you would break social convention and risk public embarrassment? Who loves you so much that they would throw the rule book out the window just to make sure you were healed?

Do you see the power of community in this story? These four friends model love, motivation, creativity, and tenacity in epic fashion. They empower their friend by walking with him . . . actually walking for him. They bring their buddy to the source of healing and place him before the only One who can restore a broken life. They enter the scene like a giant auger and drill through every obstacle between them and Jesus. Have you ever wished you had friends like that? Have you ever loved with such reckless abandon?

Notice the man on the mat. He allows others to minister to him and provide for him. He let them become his human chariot and demolition crew. They did for him what he could not do for himself, and he accepted their gift.

What a beautiful picture of teamwork, partnership, the body of Christ, family. What a vivid picture of the spiritual reality that in our weakness, one way God shows his strength is through the arms of others. In this case, they are literally carrying their friend. In other situations God simply chooses to let the resources, muscle, compassion, and care of others become ours.

God offers us a surprising source of strength through community. There are simply times we need people to carry us. We can't do it. We lack the strength, ability, or drive. In those moments God will often bestow the gift of community. Others come to our side, pick up our mat (with us on it), and carry us to the One who can heal, restore, and love us to health.

I remember the day as if it were yesterday. I will never forget it. I woke up and prepared my heart for a day like none other. I would conduct the funeral service for my mother, Patricia Ann Harney. The one who bore me in her womb, pressed me out of her body and into the air of this world, and loved me every day of my life. She was five foot no inches tall, red-headed, and cared for others with a compassion I have rarely seen in another human. I loved her and she loved me. On this day I would stand before family and friends and lead a service to honor her, share the story of Jesus, and say good-bye to my mother.

The next day I would preach my first service at Shoreline Community Church in Monterey. I was their new lead pastor and was committed to be there for my first weekend of worship services. What I did not expect was that a group of church members and leaders would get on a plane and fly the 350 miles to Fountain Valley, California. They did not know my mom. They had never met her. They knew me, a little. But when I stood up to lead the service and looked into the faces of these new friends, I felt supported, uplifted, loved. They reached down to my mat of sorrow and picked me up. They carried me through that service with their prayers and love. I did not know how much I needed them until I felt them dig through the roof and lower me to Jesus. This moment bound our hearts together.

About a year later one of those same men was preparing to have a surgery on his neck that could have left him paralyzed. I had the privilege of coming to his side, bending down, and helping pick up the mat he was on. I was able to pray, love, encourage, and walk with him through a time he could not carry himself.

As we travel through this life, we are always on the mat being carried by others, or we are walking as we carry the mat of someone in need. These are the options God gives.

The powerful say, "I am a mat carrier!" They don't need others to carry them. They can handle life's challenges on their own.

The powerless say, "I live on the mat." They believe that others exist to take care of them. They buy into the lie that they have nothing to offer.

The *empowered* have learned the rhythm of being on the mat in seasons of loss, pain, sickness, and struggle. They let the power of God flow from heaven and through the arms of ordinary people. They know that in their weakness, God brings them strength through friends, family, and even an occasional stranger. They also love the seasons when they are strong enough to stand and help carry the mat of someone who is hurting and discouraged. In these moments they delight as they feel the presence of the Holy Spirit, the power of the Father, and the very grace and healing of Jesus flow through their arms as they become a mat carrier.

A paralyzed man came to Jesus on a mat carried by four friends who cared about him. He left walking on his own two feet. This man who had watched the world walk past him as he lay flat on his back now stood up, at the command of Jesus. He picked up his mat. And, he went home!

I wonder if he ever helped carry the mat of a person in need after that day. I suspect he did!

From the Heart of the Paralytic

Fellow Mat Carrier,

Have you ever looked back and taken notice of how many times you were carried in this life? Parents and grandparents carried you for a long time and kept you safe. Friends have carried you emotionally and spiritually through rough times. People in your church who love Jesus have supported you and lifted your mat through prayer and care more times than you know.

If you could see and recognize how often God has unleashed his power and grace as he lifted you up through the arms of the people in your life, you would be amazed. You would find yourself noticing people on their mat of loss, pain, loneliness, depression, isolation, crisis, or busyness and your heart would break. You would want to help carry their load.

Remember when you have been carried. Humble your heart and let others carry you through the hard times. And let the grace and power of Jesus course through your soul and your arms as you help lift up people in their hard times and as you carry them to the only One who can heal and place them on their feet.

▸▸ **Walk with the Paralytic** and learn more of his journey of being empowered as you read Luke 5:17–26 and Mark 2:1–12.

Paul and Timothy

Climbing in Community

And the things you have heard me say in the presence of many witnesses entrust to reliable people who will also be qualified to teach others.

2 Timothy 2:2

One Sunday I preached about the importance of having people in our life who help us grow in spiritual maturity. In the same message I talked about having people who need our help as they grow in faith. To illustrate this idea, I asked two men to join me on the platform.

I had the founding pastor of the church, Howie Hugo, come up and stand on the top of the stage and asked him to grab one of my hands as tightly as he could and not let go. I stood two stairs below Howie. As I spoke, the picture became clear—this wise and seasoned leader was helping me upward. Like climbers on a mountain, he locked on to me and was pulling me higher. People connected with this image because Howie is a decade older than me. I meet with Howie for breakfast regularly and ask questions about leadership, ministry, the Monterey community, and the congregation we both serve. He shares wisdom and insights, and he often tells me where the land mines are before I step on them!

This was more than a sermon illustration. It was a picture of my life. God uses Howie to encourage and bless me and speak wisdom into my life and ministry. He also has seven children and he often encourages me as a dad and husband. You could see the congregation's appreciation for the picture unfolding in front of them. I declared my need to be mentored, to be blessed, and to receive counsel from a wiser and more seasoned man of God.

Next, I asked Jonathan Ryan to join Howie and me on the platform. Jonathan is our worship arts pastor and he is a couple of decades younger than me. I locked hands with him as he stood on the floor level of the worship center. I talked with the congregation about how I meet regularly with Jonathan and invest in his life. I encourage him as a leader in the church, but also as a husband and a young father. By God's grace, I am a source of encouragement, instruction, and spiritual strength in Jon's life. For a number of years I have been given the honor of mentoring this gifted young man.

Do you get the picture? Can you see the three of us standing there, hands locked together? This is a picture of a mature and balanced spiritual life. God has placed people in my life who are wiser in faith and who have more experience than I do. They are higher up the mountain, and with strength and grace, God uses them to take my hand and help lead me upward. They have a stabilizing role in my life and I would not be the man I am without them. I am deeply thankful for the people who invest the time and energy it takes to help me succeed in life and serve God faithfully.

I am also called to help those who are a few steps behind me on their journey of spiritual growth. I have the honor of locking hands with them and helping them forward. This is a great joy, but it also takes intentionality, time, prayer, and sacrifice.

This is our walk of faith.

Look back a couple thousand years and you will discover that the exact same picture is painted for us in the life of the apostle

Paul. He had people take his hand when he became a follower of Jesus, and they helped him grow and press forward. God placed Barnabas in the life of Paul to help the passionate new Christian up the mountain of faith.[1] As Paul grew in his love for Jesus and understanding of Christianity, he in turn took the hand of many young leaders and mentored them. One of these men, Timothy, became the leader of the church in Ephesus at a young age, and Paul grabbed his hand and kept leading him, investing in the life of this gifted young man.

Paul's friendship and leadership was more than just downloading a bunch of leadership and theological information. Their hearts were bound together. The older apostle referred to Timothy as his "dear son."[2] Timothy accompanied Paul on missionary journeys and received extensive and consistent training for ministry. Timothy would travel as a representative for Paul and minister on his behalf. When we read Paul's words about Timothy, we see an amazing level of trust and confidence in this young man. With time Timothy was entrusted with the leadership of a church in Ephesus, a cultural center of the ancient world. Paul loved Timothy like family as he called him to take the hands of others and help them along as well.

In one sentence, one simple exhortation inspired by the Holy Spirit of God, Paul called Timothy and every follower of Jesus to a lifestyle of locked hands. We should always live connected to three generations and be looking to a fourth. Read these words of the apostle Paul again. Notice the four generations of locked hands and hearts:

> And the things you have heard me say in the presence of many witnesses entrust to reliable people who will also be qualified to teach others. (2 Tim. 2:2)

Do you see each of the four generations?

Generation 1—*Paul*, speaking truth in the presence of many witnesses.

Generation 2—*Timothy*, receiving instruction and encouragement from Paul.

Generation 3—*Reliable people*, instructed by Timothy in the truth and godly living.

Generation 4—*Those influenced* by these reliable and qualified teachers.

Now, look at your life. You are standing on the mountain of faith, and you know you did not get where you are alone. Who held your hand and helped you forward? Was it a parent, grandparent, Sunday school teacher, youth leader, or some other person who loves and walks with Jesus? Who has God placed in your life to have this role right now? How are they helping and influencing your walk with Jesus in positive and life-giving ways? Picture a person in your mind and stop to thank God, right now. Imagine them holding your hand and helping you over the rugged and challenging terrain of this life. Know that they are part of God's plan for your spiritual maturity.

Then, think about the people God has placed in your life who are younger in faith and who need a helping hand. Who has God called you to mentor and invest in? Whose hand are you holding, or whose hand should you be holding? Ask for the strength of the Holy Spirit to fill you and God's wisdom to guide you. Pray for a life invested in the spiritual growth of others.

Do you want to make it up the mountain of faith in a healthy way? Don't travel alone. Invite God to grow you in spiritual maturity through wiser and more seasoned Christians. At the same time, lock hands with some people who need a boost up and support along the way. There is no better way to walk through this journey of faith.

The powerful take one of their "mighty hands" and lock on to others as they heave them forward. They try to help lots of people grow stronger in life and faith. Their other hand is empty. They are not letting anyone help them. They function like their strength can carry many others in times of need, but they themselves don't require the anchor and support that comes from people ahead of them. Eventually, with the weight of helping so many others up the mountain, they grow weary and fall backward under the sheer burden of caring for so many in need. Sometimes, those they are helping end up falling with them.

The powerless have many people they rely on. Lots of kind-hearted believers extend a hand and they grab on, over and over. They live with one hand extended upward and are very comfortable letting people help them because they feel too weak to climb the mountain in their own strength. Sadly, their other hand is empty. They can't look back down the mountain and see that there are others in need that they could actually help. Or, they look back down the mountain, see people with great needs, but never offer a hand because they are so profoundly aware of their own frailties and weaknesses. They do not realize that God wants to use them to help others grow in faith and become more mature as Christians.

The *empowered* have their right and left hand tightly locked to the hands of others. They reach up and let mature Christians help them forward as they walk with Jesus. They are profoundly aware of their own need and humbly let God strengthen them through his family. In addition, with the joy of God beating in their heart, they reach back and help others forward. They rejoice as they see God use them to help people grow in faith. They dare to believe that their life can become a conduit of God's power to people who are younger in their walk with Jesus. Empowered people have adopted a biblical lifestyle of locked hands. They have discovered that an empowered life comes when both of their hands are locked tightly to the hands of others.

From the Heart of Timothy

Dear Members of God's Family,

We belong to each other. We need one another. None of us can make it alone. We really are brothers and sisters in faith.

The climb is steep, the obstacles are many, and the terrain is treacherous. Look at your right hand. Who is holding it? Who has God placed in your life to help you stand strong and grow to look and live more like Jesus? Grab their hand. Don't be prideful. Listen to their wisdom, ask for their prayers, and let the love of the Father flow into your heart through them. These godly brothers and sisters are a gift!

Look at your left hand. Is it full or empty? Who are you helping, supporting, praying for, encouraging, challenging, and keeping accountable? Who are you helping forward on the journey of faith? Keep investing in these people. Love them like a brother or sister. Let the very power and strength of God pour from your life to theirs. Know that God has placed you in their life, and he intends to use you to infuse his blessing, grace, and hope into the life of another human being.

What an honor! What a privilege! Don't take it lightly.

▸▸ **Walk with Paul and Timothy** and learn more of the journey of being empowered through locked hands by reading 1 and 2 Timothy.

Ruth and Naomi

Forging a Family

Don't urge me to leave you or to turn back from you. Where you go I will go, and where you stay I will stay. Your people will be my people and your God my God. Where you die I will die, and there I will be buried. May the LORD deal with me, be it ever so severely, if even death separates you and me.

Ruth 1:16–17

Her stomach was empty because famine had descended on the land of Judah.[1] There was no food to be found in the city of Bethlehem, and famine in the ancient world could be a death sentence for those who were poor and had no reserves. As Naomi traveled away from her homeland and toward the foreign country of Moab, she was also full. At her side was her husband Elimelek, and close on their heels were the boys, Mahlon and Kilion. Family fills the heart even when the stomach growls. So this little family traveled east looking for work, food, and a future. As they traveled, Naomi, the matriarch, was both empty and full.

The land of Moab became their home, and they began to make a life for themselves. The famine continued back in Judah, but there was enough work and food to make ends meet in their new land of residence. Yes, they were foreigners, but they had each other. Then, tragedy struck. The Bible does not give commentary, explanation, or the slightest detail. We simply read the words, "Now Elimelek, Naomi's husband, died."[2] Her heart was emptied as the man of her life was suddenly and unexpectedly wrenched from her arms. A part of her soul became vacant in a way that only a widow understands.

In the ancient world where Naomi lived, there were no social services, no community care programs, and no safety net for widows. To be a single woman in the ancient world was to be utterly unprotected. The only hope was to marry again. Or to have a son who would protect and provide.

Though Naomi's heart carried an empty place in the loss of her husband, she still had her two sons. They both married good Moabite girls and forged a family. Mother Naomi, the boys, and their wives, Orpah and Ruth. For about a decade the family lived in Moab and made ends meet. With sons and two daughters-in-law, Naomi's heart began to fill up again.

Then, like a storm that descends and hits with no warning, disaster struck again. In one line of biblical text, without detail or backstory, we read, "Both Mahlon and Kilion also died."[3] With one swipe of the pen, only six words in the English language, we read that Naomi, Orpah, and Ruth were all alone in a world hostile to widows. Naomi had lost her husband and sons, and she was a foreigner far from home. Orpah and Ruth were young widows with no idea what the future would hold.

In moments like these, some people can decide their only hope is to make it on their own. They can look at the emptiness of their heart and be tempted to lock off a part of their soul to make sure they never feel that kind of pain again. Some steel their face to the storms of life and press on in their own strength, keeping the people in their life at arm's length.

These are the times when wise people discover that community, friendship, family, and the church are desperately needed. We are not powerful enough to make it on our own. What we need in times of pain and loss is deep connection to people who will love God and love us as well. The God of heaven wants to use the people around us as a conduit of his grace and care.

Of course no one could take the place of Elimelek in the heart of Naomi. No one could fill the empty place in a mother's heart when she lost not one but two sons. She was brokenhearted and desperate. To her surprise, the strength Naomi needed would come wrapped in human flesh. A Moabite woman would be the conduit of grace poured from heaven into the empty and broken heart of Naomi.

The news came from Judah—weather patterns had changed, rain was falling, crops were growing again. The famine was over! Naomi began her journey back to Bethlehem in Judah. She could remember the trip she had taken more than a decade before. At that time her stomach was empty but her heart was full. Now, as she traveled home, her heart was empty but her stomach was full. She, like all of us, would have traded those two realities in a moment, if she could.

On her return journey, there was no man at her side. There were no sons following on her heels. But there were two widows following Naomi, trying to figure out their future. Orpah and Ruth had become family to Naomi through their marriages to her sons. They were now husbandless and vulnerable. They had grown to love their mother-in-law, but the prospect of moving to a foreign land as a widow was daunting and fear-filled.

Naomi spoke tenderly to these two women who had become so dear to her. She released them and encouraged them to head back to their family of origin and the land of their birth. Maybe there they could find protection and provision through some other man who might become part of their life.

Tears were shed and Naomi kissed them both and sent them on their way. Orpah turned and began the walk back to her family home. Ruth did not budge. Something had happened in her heart while she was part of this Jewish family. She had grown to love Naomi. But, more important, she had come to know the God of Israel. Ruth discovered that the idols made of stone, wood, and metal that she had grown up worshiping were vain and empty. They could not and did not fill her. When she met Yahweh, the one true God of the universe, she was saturated with grace and filled like never before.

Naomi looked squarely at Ruth and let her know that there was nothing she could offer her. No other son. No promise of provision. No guaranteed hope for the future. But Ruth replied with words that must have healed the heart of Naomi and inspired her as they have every generation since they were uttered:

> Don't urge me to leave you or to turn back from you. Where you go I will go, and where you stay I will stay. Your people will be my people and your God my God. Where you die I will die, and there I will be buried. May the LORD deal with me, be it ever so severely, if even death separates you and me. (Ruth 1:16–17)

Empowering words spoken by a woman who would become part of the lineage of the Messiah, Jesus Christ.[4] Sometimes God chooses to pour power into our lives through people, surprising people. Just imagine you were in Naomi's place. Your husband is gone, your sons have suddenly passed, you are about to walk the dusty desert roads back to your homeland with a heart as dry and arid as the path below your feet . . . empty.

Then, God places a Ruth right next to you. You tell this person, "I'm OK, go on your way. Take care of yourself. I'll make it."

But they don't leave. They don't walk away. They look at you and speak words of grace, power, hope, and trust in God. You realize you are not alone. You are not truly empty. God has put someone in your life to declare truth and infuse in your soul the rock-solid assurance that not only is this person there for you, but more importantly, God is with you!

In your emptiness, God fills you. In your aridness, he refreshes you. Where you are powerless, he infuses you with energy. You know, you just know, that you can make the next step and begin your walk back home.

When Naomi traveled from Bethlehem to Moab, her heart was full with the love of family. A husband, two sons, and a future. What seemed like a lifetime later, when she walked back toward

Bethlehem in Judah, she discovered that even with all of her loss, she was not alone. She was not empty. God gave her Ruth to walk at her side, and the one true God used this young Moabite girl to remind Naomi, in the midst of her pain, that she would never be alone because God would never leave her.

The powerful face trials, pain, and loss, and press on. In their own strength they resolve to make it by themselves and never rely on people who might leave them, let them down, or be taken from them.

Powerless people decide they can't make it home so they sit on the side of the road in despair.

The *empowered* discover that their strength will not be enough to carry them through the journey of life and all the way back home. But God has not left them alone. They look to their right and left and rejoice when they learn that the Maker of the universe loves them so much that he has placed people near them who will pray, love, help, and fortify them along the way. They discover that God has invited them into a family of faith and these people are one of God's best sources of continual and amazing strength.

From the Heart of Naomi

My dear Sisters and Brothers,

Is the road you are walking dry and dusty? Does your heart feel parched and your soul arid?

Don't stop walking! Press on. You are not alone. God sees your tears. He is still with you. He loves you so much that he places people in your life to bring grace and strength, wisdom, and tender care.

Don't push these people away. Don't send them home. Let them love you. Allow the power of heaven to flow into your life through each of them. Look into their eyes and discover that these dear people are messengers of the mighty God.

As the Lord gives you strength, love them back. In their arid seasons allow the refreshment of God to flow through you into their lives. If you do this, you will never be alone . . . unless you choose to be.

God is with you. He has invited you into a family of faith. Let this truth empower you as you take your next step on your way home.

▶▶ **Walk with Naomi** and learn more about her journey of being empowered by community as you read the book of Ruth.

10

Lois, Eunice, and Timothy

The Blessing of a Spiritual Legacy

> I thank God, whom I serve, as my ancestors did, with a clear conscience, as night and day I constantly remember you in my prayers. Recalling your tears, I long to see you, so that I may be filled with joy. I am reminded of your sincere faith, which first lived in your grandmother Lois and in your mother Eunice and, I am persuaded, now lives in you also.
>
> 2 Timothy 1:3–5

I have to be honest, sometimes I get upset with Christians who complain about how they "had to go to church when they were growing up." I feel sad when I hear believers grumble because their parents "compelled them to read the Bible and pray when they were little." When I hear followers of Jesus whine about how they wasted the Sunday mornings of their childhood going to church or how their parents' Christian faith was "imposed on them," I get frustrated.

I would have been overjoyed to have just one person kneel next to my bed when I was a baby or little boy and pray for me. I would have rejoiced if anyone had given me a Bible and told me the stories of faith. When I was afraid at night and thought there were monsters under my bed, it would have been comforting to have someone tell me about the God of love, power, and grace who was watching over me.

I had none of these.

I never went to church. Never heard a Bible story. Never saw someone pray. I can't even remember seeing or holding a Bible until I became a Christian as a teenager. Into my mid teenage years I had no idea that Christmas and Easter were religious holidays. I did not have a single friend, as far as I can remember, who went to any church.

When I received Jesus at almost sixteen years of age, a young college student who volunteered with the youth group at the Garden Grove Community Church generously bought me a hardback Revised Standard Version Bible, with study notes by Harold Lindsell. The beginning of my discipleship training was raw and simple. The young man who gave me my first Bible said, "This is the Word of God. You are supposed to read it every day and do what it says!"

I took him at his word and committed from 6:00 a.m. until noon every day, for the rest of the summer, to read this strange and wonderful book. My parents were baffled by my behavior and astonished when I told them that I would not answer any phone calls or come to the front door until noon. A few months later I went to the youth volunteer who gave me my Bible and asked him, "What am I supposed to read next?" He looked at me with a quizzical expression on his face and inquired, "How far did you get?" I said, "I finished it, and I read all the little notes on the bottom of the page too." He stared at me for a moment, paused, and gave me my second assignment in my training as a follower of Jesus, "Read it again!" I have been following these same instructions for thirty-five years.

More than three decades later, there are times I stand in front of the congregation I serve with a lump in my throat and tears in my eyes. I plead with the young people, "Thank your parents for loving you enough to bring you to church. Don't fight them. I wish I had what you have. Appreciate the fact that your parents read the Bible and encourage you to do the same. Don't resent it. Thank God that your parents teach you about God's love, share their stories of Jesus's presence in their lives, and seek to live in the power of the Holy Spirit." Then I tell them my story. I let them know that I would have loved to have gone to church as a young boy. I wish I had grown up with parents who prayed for me and did their best to point me to Jesus. I let the young people know they have a gift that I can never reclaim . . . years of learning about the Christian faith as a young person.

I exhort parents, "Share your faith with your children. Don't buy the garbage and lies of our culture that says a dad or mom should not strongly teach the Christian faith to their children." The truth is, we are all sinners. We will not find our way to God on our own. God is seeking us like a lost sheep, coin, and child.[1] God chooses to use parents, grandparents, and other family members to influence the next generation and point them to Jesus.

In Deuteronomy 6, right after the "Shema,"[2] the great creed of Israel, we read that parents are called by God to intentionally and consistently pass on biblical faith to the next generation. Notice the progression in the passage. First, a parent must be growing to love God with their heart, soul, and strength. Then, they can naturally pass this faith on to their children.

> Hear, O Israel: The LORD our God, the LORD is one. Love the LORD your God with all your heart and with all your soul and with all your strength. These commandments that I give you today are to be on your hearts. Impress them on your children. Talk about them when you sit at home and when you walk along the road, when you lie down and when you get up. Tie them as symbols on your hands and bind them on your foreheads. Write them on the doorframes of your houses and on your gates. (Deut. 6:4–9)

A brief but beautiful example of this can be found in one short passage. The apostle Paul was writing to his son in the faith, Timothy. He remembered that Timothy's mother and grandmother shared in the glorious ministry of passing on their faith to the next generation. With time, Timothy became a pastor and leader in the church. It was his mother and grandmother who handed him the legacy of love for God and the truth of Scripture that helped shape his heart and life.

> I thank God, whom I serve, as my ancestors did, with a clear conscience, as night and day I constantly remember you in my prayers. Recalling your tears, I long to see you, so that I may be filled with joy. I am reminded of your sincere faith, which first lived in your grandmother Lois and in your mother Eunice and, I am persuaded, now lives in you also. (2 Tim. 1:3–5)

This brief mention of family faith does not spell out the exact patterns and behaviors of Timothy's grandmother Lois or his mother, Eunice. What we can know is that they both had authentic and personal faith and they let it show. Timothy was shaped by the faith of two generations of godly women.

His family life would have been guided by the teachings of Scripture. His home would have been filled with prayer. His weeks were punctuated with times of gathered worship where God's people would sing, learn, and celebrate the one true God who made the heavens and the earth. Timothy learned the stories of great people of faith like Abraham, Moses, Esther, and Jonah. He heard the psalms recited and sung. Faith was in the air he breathed, and Timothy drew it deeply into his lungs and soul and became a great leader in the early church.

Just imagine the joy and pride in the hearts of Lois and Eunice when Timothy became a pastor and leader in the city of Ephesus. They could look on, support him in prayer, continue to speak into his life, and celebrate that their years of sharing God's Word with this young man were now producing a harvest for the kingdom of God.

The place of solid and bold family faith becomes more urgent as our world moves farther from God. In modern culture, morality and biblical ethics are being crushed to dust and swept off the back porch. A whole new generation is growing up that does not know right from wrong. Truth is seen as relative and absolutes have gone the way of VHS tapes, waterbeds, and phone booths. This generation is in desperate need of parents, grandparents, and extended family who will teach the truth of the Scriptures, with words and godly lifestyle, to the next generation.

I was reminded about the importance of this when I encountered a high school student who grew up in a home with no faith and deep dysfunction. His father was harsh toward both him and his mother. To add greater confusion to the situation, his dad also happened to be in a high profile job that demanded great respect. His dad eventually left the family, and this young man was being raised by a mom who was living with no clear moral boundaries or sense of right and wrong.

This young man, Karl (not his real name), became a follower of Jesus. He was only sixteen, but his heart was set aflame by the grace and presence of the living Christ. He was changed! He wanted to walk closely with the Savior but had no idea what this looked like, in any tangible way. And he had a girlfriend who was not a Christian and they seemed very close.

I remember asking Karl, "What do you think God would say to a young person like you about being sexually active outside of marriage?" He looked at me with firm and absolute confidence in his voice and said, "I think God is fine with young people having sex as long as they care about each other and use protection." His response did not shock me. Instead, it simply confirmed the reality of how his generation thinks. Many people, even new believers in Jesus, are void of moral boundaries.

I did not argue with Karl. I refrained from telling him he was wrong. I simply gave him a handful of Bible passages on the topic of sexuality and encouraged him to read them. Then I said, "After you read these passages, reflect on one question: What does the Bible teach about sex outside of marriage?"

He quickly agreed to do this and seemed excited about the assignment.

The next time I saw Karl, I asked him, "So what do you think? What does God have to say about sex before marriage?" With a confidence and boldness that was becoming characteristic of this new follower of Jesus, Karl leveled his eyes at me and personalized his answer: "I need to stop having sex with my girlfriend!" He went on to tell me that the Bible was very clear about this (which, by the way, I already knew). Karl assured me that he was going to tell his girlfriend this right away and that they would not be having sex anymore.

Wow! This is the power of the truth in a truth-starved world. When one generation challenges the next to dig into God's Word, start to pray, and grow in faith, lives are radically changed.

As an addendum to Karl's story, a few weeks later his mother contacted me. She wanted to meet and talk because she was concerned about some of the changes in her son. It turned out that after her divorce she had not remarried, but she had invited a series of different men to live with her and her son.

You might already be ahead of me and be able to guess what happened next and why I got the phone call from Karl's mom.

She told me that her teenage son had sat down with her and explained what the Bible says about how she was living. He challenged her to stop living with men until she was married. He also let her know about his commitment to stop having sex with his girlfriend.

When I met with Karl's mom, she was more fascinated than upset. She was amazed at the change in her son and his boldness. My wife and I became friends with her in the coming year, and her heart began to open to the gospel and the message of Jesus. Karl's faith began to impact his mother and it was a joy to see.

God offers each of us a spiritual legacy. Sometimes it is blood relatives like in Timothy's story. His mother and grandmother passed on a spiritual heritage that transformed his life and future. At other times it is a person who is not related through bloodlines but through the family of God. In either case, God loves to empower us through people who can become spiritual parents and influencers.

Powerful people see their journey of faith as exactly that—*their* journey. They don't notice how God has used others to grow, teach, and empower them. They fail to see the beautiful impact of a spiritual legacy.

Those who feel powerless might take note of how God helps them through family members and Christian friends, but they don't recognize the potential for God to use them as a blessing to others.

The *empowered* have a unique ability to recognize the many ways God has impacted their life of faith through parents, grandparents, extended family, and members of their church family. They are grateful and want to pass this legacy forward. So, they look for ways to become a channel of God's truth, wisdom, and encouragement to the next generation.

From the Hearts of Lois and Eunice

To Parents and Grandparents,

You have a sacred trust. God has placed children and grandchildren in your life. This is no accident. You have a ministry, a calling, a divine opportunity. Never underestimate the importance of your role.

Keep praying for your children and grandchildren, no matter how old they get. Keep crying out to God on their behalf, even if they are running away from God's plan for their life.

Share your stories of faith. With joy, tell the next generation about the greatness of God, his miracles in your life, and answered prayers.

Read the Scriptures and tell your children and grandchildren what God is teaching you. Share stories of faith from the Bible, even if you have told them countless times before.

Never grow weary, don't ever stop, press on. For the sake of the gospel and the need for the next generation to know the love

92

of Jesus, let your light shine. In your own home, in your family, let your faith be seen and heard.

▸▸ Walk with Lois, Eunice, and Timothy and learn more of their journey of being empowered as a family of faith by reading 1 and 2 Timothy.

11

The Woman at the Well

From Outcast to Embraced

Come, see a man who told me everything I ever did.

John 4:29

She dropped the bucket down the well and pulled it up again. She had done this countless times since she was a little girl. One of the tasks of women during that time of history and in that part of the world was to draw the water that was life for all who lived in that arid and desolate land.

Walk to the well, draw water, carry it back to town, and do it again . . . and again . . . and again.

The problem was and is, water never fully satisfies. Sure, it does for a moment, for an hour, but by the next day the body craves and cries out for more. So, this nameless woman from Samaria went again to drop her bucket down the well, pull it up, and collect the water she desperately needed.

Her whole life felt like a search for fresh water to quench the thirsting deep inside. It was more than just water from a well. She had dropped a lot of buckets into a lot of wells, but her soul was still arid, empty, and crying out for something to satiate her parched heart.

She threw the bucket of her heart down the marriage well and pulled it up. Would this relationship satisfy? Would this man love her? Would marriage quench the longing so deep inside? We don't have all the details, but the relationship ended and she was not satisfied. So the bucket went down into the marriage well again, and again, and again, and one more time! Five husbands, five shattered relationships, and one empty and broken woman with a heart as scorched as the dusty roads of Sychar.

By the sixth man she did not even bother with the wedding festivities. She was just living with him. No need for formalities. Just another bucket tossed down another well and a heart still thirsting for acceptance, love, and hope. Each day she went to the well and drew water, only to be thirsty by the next sunrise. Each night she would place the bucket of her heart into the hands of her most recent relationship and discover that the momentary refreshment would evaporate and her heart would once again be empty.

On one life-changing day, under the heat of the noonday sun, this Samaritan woman came again to the very well from which the great patriarch of the faith, Jacob, had drawn water. She approached the well she had walked to countless times before. She came to draw the water needed for her household.

This day was different.

This time everything would change.

On this day she met a man different from any she had ever encountered.

As Jesus was traveling with his disciples, their journey forced them to cut through the land of Samaria. In those days, the Jewish people and the Samaritans avoided each other at all costs. There was no love between them. Though they had history as worshipers of Yahweh and they shared some ancient bloodlines, conflict centuries before still left scars and resentment. Jews and Samaritans would not interact unless absolutely necessary. In addition, men did not converse with women in public. To top it off, a Jewish rabbi would not talk theology and Scripture with any woman.

Jesus, a Jewish rabbi, sat resting near Jacob's well as the woman from Samaria approached. The woman came and did what she had done every day as long as she could remember. She dropped her bucket down the well and pulled up some water. She did it automatically, without thinking—it was like breathing, it was what she did.

Jesus broke the tense silence that hung over the well. He asked if she would give him a drink. The Jewish rabbi asked a favor of the sinful Samaritan woman. She stated what both of them knew with absolute certainty. This sort of thing never happened. You can read between the lines and hear the tone of disbelief in her voice. "You are a Jew, I am a Samaritan. You are a man, I am a woman. You are a rabbi, I am a nobody!"[1] She was in shock. She knew that for a Jew to touch or drink from a container of a Samaritan would make them "unclean." The Jews believed that contact with certain groups of people would actually spiritually contaminate them and they would have to go through a process of ritual cleansing. And guess what, Samaritans were high up on the list of people who would make Jews unclean.[2]

There was even a prayer in the ancient Jewish world that went like this: "God, I thank you that I was not born a woman, a Samaritan, or a dog."[3] But the way Jesus engaged this woman was tender, gracious, kind, and utterly countercultural. So the woman told Jesus that she could not believe he would even consider asking this favor of her.

Jesus spun the tables and told her that if she really knew him and all that he was about, she would have actually come to him and requested that he do her a favor and draw water for her. This was even more unheard of. But now he had her attention!

What followed was an in-depth theological conversation about the source of living water, true worship, and the Messiah. We don't know if this conversation lasted minutes or hours, but we know that something happened in the course of this encounter. A thirsty, broken, lonely, bucket-dropping Samaritan woman finally found what her soul was yearning for. Somehow, her dry and broken heart was healed. Her loneliness was gone. Her life, for the first time, made sense and felt right. Her days of dropping buckets down any and every kind of well that gave any promise of happiness were over!

She had dropped the bucket of her heart down a new well and drew up water that refreshed every part of her arid soul. She found the forgiveness of Jesus, the Living Water. She was healed, saved, born again!

In their conversation Jesus did something that seems strange at first glance. He asked her to go to town and invite her husband to come join the conversation. She tentatively declared what Jesus already knew: she did not have a husband. Jesus then doubled down on the invasive and culturally inappropriate confrontation. His words were not angry but firm, clear, and piercing in truth:

> You are right when you say you have no husband. The fact is, you have had five husbands, and the man you now have is not your husband. What you have just said is quite true. (John 4:17–18)

Ouch! Why would Jesus speak this way to a woman who is already broken and empty? The answer is simple: Jesus is the truth and his truth is what sets us free, even when it hurts. Only Jesus and the truth he brings provide a lasting source of the salvation, freedom, and the soul-quenching water we all need.

Jesus held up the mirror of her life and let the woman see herself. He let her know that he, the Messiah, knew everything about her. No secrets. No hidden sins. No skeletons in the closet. Everything was out in the open, on the table, and Jesus knew her through and through. What this woman learned was that Jesus knew everything about her and he still loved her! This Rabbi Messiah could see right through her sin-soiled soul, and he was ready to draw living water for her, wash her clean, and fill her to overflowing.

When the disciples returned, they were shocked to see Jesus engaged in an intimate and deeply theological conversation with a Samaritan woman. But they were getting used to Jesus breaking the cultural norms, so they said nothing.

What the woman did next reveals the new condition of her soul. She left her water container and headed back to town. This bucket she had carried countless times to the well and back home again. This physical object that had become a metaphor for her seeking to fill her dry and barren life. She left it behind as if to say, "I am refreshed for the first time in my life! I am forgiven. I am so full that I can overflow into the lives of others." And that is what she did.

The five-times-married, shacking-up-with-another-man Samaritan woman headed into town and shared her story of forgiveness, transformation, and soul refreshment. She began with these words: "He told me everything I ever did."[4] The people in the town of Sychar knew all about the many things she had done. There was a reason she went to the well by herself in the heat of the day instead of in the cool of the evening with the other women from town. She was an outcast, even among her own people.

Imagine how a woman might have been scorned in a small mid-American town in the 1950s if she had been through five husbands and was now living with a man but not married to him. It was even worse in the ancient world! This Samaritan woman wore a scarlet letter on her tunic and her soul. Everyone knew her story and the condition of her life.

Now she invites the people from her town to come and encounter a man who told her everything she had ever done. Can you hear her voice as she speaks of the forgiveness of Jesus? She declares to people, "This man knows *everything* about me and he still loves me. He knows *everything* and he forgives me. He knows *everything* about my history and he offered me himself as Living Water that will quench my soul forever."

What happened next was nothing short of a Holy Spirit–anointed miracle. A revival broke out in the Samaritan town of Sychar as people placed their faith in this Jewish Messiah. They believed in him because of the woman's testimony. They could see it in her eyes, hear it in her voice, she was changed. Many others came to meet Jesus and he held two days of revival meetings in Samaria. Jews would avoid Samaria like the plague, but Jesus and his disciples pitched a tent and hung out for a couple more days as people came to learn from the Rabbi and many of them placed their faith in him as Messiah and Savior. They met someone who told them everything they had ever done and he still loved them, offered forgiveness, and was ready to refresh their dry souls forever.

Powerful people own lots of buckets and they throw them down many wells. They believe that if they drop enough buckets down enough wells, they will eventually draw up something that will satisfy their empty soul. Day after day and night after night, they drop buckets into jobs, relationships, romance, material things, experiences, and countless other wells. They drink and drink and drink but never experience the refreshment their heart needs.

Powerless people have grown weary. They have decided that there is no reason to keep dropping another bucket down another well. They have given up. They are not refreshed, their soul is arid, and they don't even bother anymore.

Empowered people have come to Jesus, the source of living water. They have dared to ask him for a drink and he has filled them with eternal refreshment. Empowered people are no longer dropping the bucket of their heart down the endless wells the world offers. They have come to Jesus, the One who knows everything they have ever done, they have looked into his eyes, and they have learned he still loves them.

From the Heart of a Nameless Woman

Fellow Bucket Carrier,

It is time. Stop dropping your bucket down well after well after well. Stop looking for satisfaction, refreshment, love, and life in wells that only satisfy for a moment, a day, or a night.

Come to Jesus and receive his living water. Come to Jesus and hear his voice. Listen as he tells you that he knows everything about you. He knows your pain, your shame, your brokenness, your fears, and your weariness. He knows every well you have dropped a bucket into and he knows it did not satisfy your heart.

Look into the eyes of this Jesus, this Savior, this Messiah, and you will see that he knows you and still loves you. He wants you to know that there is only one source of living water that will refresh your soul forever. Drop your bucket down just one more well, the well of Jesus.

What will happen? You will be saved, healed, and refreshed. You will also overflow. The living water of Jesus the Christ will fill you until it pours from your life to the lives of every person you encounter.

When this happens, drop your bucket and carry it no more. The Living Water will be in you forever.

▸▸ **Walk with the Woman at the Well** and learn more of her journey of being empowered through her encounter with Jesus by reading the Gospel of John chapters 3–4.

12

Jesus and His Friends

Crushed and Poured Out, But Not Alone

Then Jesus went with his disciples to a place called Gethsemane, and he said to them, "Sit here while I go over there and pray." He took Peter and the two sons of Zebedee along with him, and he began to be sorrowful and troubled. Then he said to them, "My soul is overwhelmed with sorrow to the point of death. Stay here and keep watch with me."

Matthew 26:36–38

The shadow of the cross loomed thick over the Garden of Gethsemane and the heart of Jesus. The Savior knew, from before time, that he would walk the hill of Calvary. He entered human history to take the nails in his flesh, bear the sins of the world, receive the righteous judgment we deserved, and die in our place. Jesus, this man of sorrows, was the Lamb of God who takes away the sins of the world. He was, and is, the Lamb slain before the foundations of the earth. He came as the final sacrifice and he came willingly.

As Jesus walked with his friends toward this secluded olive grove, sorrow was etched into his face. There was heaviness in each slow and deliberate step.

When they arrived at their familiar meeting place in the garden, the sky was dark and so was the look in Jesus's eyes. The Lord of glory was preparing for battle. He was going to war. This time of prayer with his closest friends would be an affirmation of why Jesus came and what he would do in the coming hours.

As he had done on many occasions before, Jesus asked Peter, James, and John to stay close to him in this critical time of spiritual engagement. He invited them to watch, pray, and partner with him in one of the most excruciating moments of his life. Jesus, God in human flesh, admitted to his friends, "My soul is overwhelmed with sorrow to the point of death."[1]

Jesus could have gone to the garden alone, but he invited his closest friends to be with him. The Savior could have prayed by himself, but he desired community in this intense time of being pressed out and crushed. The Lord could have been sorrowful in seclusion, but he opened his heart to a group of brothers who had walked with him. Jesus asked if they would share his load and be near him in this dark and painful moment.

Today the garden is more of a tourist stop than a place for quiet reflection. When my wife and I had an opportunity to visit Gethsemane during a trip to Israel, the tour guide said, as he had us pile off the bus, "Take a walk around but be back in about ten minutes so we can get to the next gathering place for our daily lesson." We were part of a group with a number of buses and each day we would all congregate for an amazing time of Bible study with a well-respected teacher. It was a meaningful trip, but some of the stops were severely abbreviated and this was one of them.

I tried to quiet my heart, reflect, and picture my Savior in this place two thousand years earlier. I tried to imagine his friends as they did their best to support Jesus in prayer and dozed in and out of consciousness.

Unfortunately, the crowds and the need to keep an eye on my watch made it difficult to draw near to God in this sacred place. As I scurried back to the bus, I felt I had missed much of the rich meaning of this garden. I looked over my shoulder as we drove away and found myself wishing I could have lingered, prayed, and reflected with greater depth in the garden.

Sometimes wishes come true.

The next day, a wonderful couple we met on the trip gave us an offer. The husband leaned over to Sherry and me as we were riding on the bus and said, "We're breaking out of here. Do you want to join us?" He had a twinkle in his eye, a smile on his face, and two extra seats in the van he had hired. I asked for a little more detail. He went on to explain that a young Christian man was coming to pick up him, his wife, and their adult kids and spouses so they could do a slower and more reflective tour of a couple of locations we had skimmed over in the past couple of days. One of those locations was the Garden of Gethsemane.

We were in!

Later that day we were back in the garden. It must have been an off time because there were no tour buses and the garden was quiet. Sherry and I, along with our new friends, had some quiet time to walk, pray, and meet with Jesus. There was a sweetness as I reflected on how Jesus would retreat to this place with close friends many times in his ministry. There was a soberness when I thought about that final night in the garden and how his closest friends slept while Jesus agonized in prayer, preparing himself to bear our sins and the Father's wrath on the cross. In a sense, I felt I was afforded time to meet with Jesus in a place where he often met with friends. In this place and time, my friendship with the Savior grew deeper.

When we finished our time of quiet reflection, our driver took us below the garden to a small cave where there was an ancient olive press. I had never seen anything quite like it. It was a huge, flat slab of stone. Almost like a thick tabletop. There was another large slab, the same size, that was suspended above the first stone. Then, there was a long, strong beam of wood attached to the top stone and suspended outward. It had three large, heavy boulders attached to the arm. The weight of these three stones would pull the two slabs together and crush olives.

Our driver explained the process of how this particular press worked. In ancient times they would spread olives all over the tabletop of the first slab of smooth stone. Then, they would hang a huge stone on the beam and it would pull the upper stone down and begin to crush the olives. The oil from this first "press" was considered the best and was used for offerings and sacred purposes like anointing. When the oil stopped flowing, they would suspend another stone from the beam, and the weight would cause the stones to crush the olives and the oil would begin to flow again. The second "press" produced oil that was used for medical and other valuable purposes. Finally, a third large stone was suspended from the beam and the weight pulled the massive flat stones together and turned what was left of the olives to pulp. This third "press" caused the last of the oil to flow. This was used for common purposes like cooking.

I stood there amazed. My mind was operating on two levels. First, I was looking at what happened below the garden in the olive pressing room. Three presses, three stones, three outpourings. At the same time I was picturing Jesus in the garden above, being pressed, crushed, and poured out for us. Three times of prayer, surrender, and crying out to the Father. He was sorrowful, overwhelmed, and his sweat became like drops of blood.[2] Somehow, as Jesus prayed, prayed, and prayed a third time, this act of surrender to the Father's will was part of his passion, suffering, and payment for our sins.

I asked our guide, "What did they do with the olives after the third press?" He said, "They threw them away—there was nothing left to use." His words went through my heart like the tip of a spear. In a new way, I could see Jesus, under the press, crushed, poured out, and emptied for us. He gave everything for the wayward children he loves. When he was done, there was nothing left to give. Nothing else could be squeezed out of him.

As Jesus walked into the garden, he knew that the agony of the cross was ahead of him. He gathered his best friends and asked them to stay with him, to watch, to pray. The Lord of the universe stumbled deeper into the garden and fell face-first onto the dirt.

He surrendered to the will of the Father. When he returned to his friends, he discovered they were dozing off. He woke them, gave a short lesson on the weakness of the flesh and the reality of temptation, and asked them to pray with him. Has it ever struck you that while Jesus was in the midst of this unthinkable spiritual battle, being crushed and poured out for our sins, he stopped to exhort and teach his disciples? What a gracious Lord!

A second and third time Jesus went and prayed. The weight was crushing. His blood flowed, not just on the cross, but in the garden. And after the third time of prayer, he was emptied, crushed, surrendered, and betrayed.

Judas, one of Jesus's closest friends, led a large crowd into the secret place of the garden and turned Jesus over to the authorities.[3] From there, the trials, a scourging, and the cross. Jesus would not let his followers fight for him or try to stop the inevitable. He was surrendered to the will of his Father. He would go to the cross and allow the final breaking, crushing, and outpouring. Salvation would be made available to all who would simply receive the broken and crushed Savior.

Powerful people face tough times in their own strength. They stand alone. The idea of calling on others to surround them, fortify them, or pray for them does not make sense to them.

Powerless people ask others to pray but forget that they have access to God as well. They feel that their prayers are not powerful or heard by God, so they look to others to carry the load.

Empowered people dare to say, "Come and pray with me. I need you. Stand with me in my time of pain and struggle." But they also fall on their face and seek God in passionate and honest prayer. They know that the arms of God are open to them and their prayers can be a powerful force when the weight of life comes crushing down.

Jesus prayed three times. But he did not pray alone. His friends, though sleepy and fickle, were with him in the garden. They did pray, but they also dozed off. Jesus lived in community, and in his deepest moments of sorrow and crushing, he invited friends to be near him.

From the Heart of Jesus

My Friend,

Don't travel through this life alone. Don't face struggles and pain in isolation. Invite others to walk with you, pray with you, and watch over you.

You say, "But my friends might let me down. They could disappoint me. They might even bail out and be absent when I need them most." You are right. This is not only possible, but, in the journey of your life, it is highly probable!

You must decide. Will you walk alone? Will you refuse the fellowship and friendship of people because they are broken, imperfect, and fall asleep when you need them the most? If this is your decision, your journey will be long and lonely.

Or will you invite flawed people to come near you in your joy and pain? Will you learn to invite ordinary human beings to come close as friends, even when they might let you down and hurt you?

Friends might betray you, doubt you, deny you, abandon you, fall asleep when you need them most, and sell you out. They just might. But you were still made for community. You need them and they need you. If you are looking for perfect friends, stop searching, they don't exist. Just do your best to be a friend and let your friends come close to you, even if they doze off in your time of need.

➤ **Walk with Jesus** and learn more about how you can draw power from community by reading Matthew 17:1–13; Mark 5:21–43; Matthew 26:36–56; Luke 22:39–46.

Resources for Living an Empowered Life

Receiving the Strength You Need Today

We live in a world where people have lots of friends they connect with on social media but not so many in the real world.

Who shows up and sits next to you when you are sick? Who would drive an hour to pick you up at the airport? How many friends do you have that would help you move a piano from one house to another? Do you have people in your life who pray for you in times of need and who do this on a regular basis? These are deep level friends. These are people with whom you experience real community.

One of God's best ways to infuse your life with power in the good times and the hard times is relationships. People are often God's conduit of grace, care, prayer, and strength.

In a culture where we stay too busy, move too fast, and connect online more than face-to-face, we need to reclaim the joy and value of human community. This takes work. It is growing more and more countercultural. It is a rare gift, but one all of our hearts and souls long to experience.

Here are some ideas, prayers, and activities that can help you experience God's power through community and friendships.

Daily Reading Guide for Week 2 of *Empowered*

Use these daily Bible readings and chapters from *Empowered* to gain a solid biblical picture of people who have experienced being empowered through community and friendships. Learn and be inspired as you enter into their story.

Day and Character	Bible Reading	Reading in *Empowered*
Day 1—A Paralytic	Luke 5 and Mark 2	Chapter 7
Day 2—Paul and Timothy	1 Timothy 1	Chapter 8
Day 3—Ruth and Naomi	Ruth 1	Chapter 9
Day 4—Lois, Eunice, and Timothy	2 Timothy 1	Chapter 10
Day 5—The Woman at the Well	John 4	Chapter 11
Weekend—Jesus and His Friends	Matthew 17:1–13; 26:36–56; Mark 5:21–43; Luke 22:39–46	Chapter 12

Prayer Guide

Take time to pray using the following prompts and ask God to empower you in fresh new ways:

- Thank Jesus for being your closest friend (even if you don't always realize it). Ask him to teach you how to be a friend who loves others as he loves you.

- Thank God for the friends in your life who have carried your mat and brought you to Jesus in the tough times.

- Pray for a friend who is going through a hard time right now. Lift up their mat by bringing them to Jesus.

- Thank God for parents, grandparents, aunts, uncles, or older siblings who have invested in your spiritual life and encouraged you to walk closely with the Savior.

- Pray that you will notice young people in the generation behind you and help them know, grow, and walk with Jesus.

- Pray for eyes to see sinful and broken people as loved by God and in need of the grace of Jesus.

- Confess where you have been judgmental and critical of people who are far from God and stuck deep in sin.

Journal and Personal Reflections

Write some of your own thoughts and reflections on the following topics and questions:

Reflect on one Christian friend who has loved and cared for you in ways that reflect the heart of Jesus. What characteristics have marked this person's life and how can you learn from their example?

_____

_____

_____

_____

_____

Who has held your hand and pulled you up the mountain of faith? How has this person helped you grow in spiritual maturity?

_____

_____

_____

_____

_____

Who are you helping grow closer to Jesus? What are one or two ways you can be more intentional and effective in helping this person grow in their faith?

_____

_____

_____

_____

_____

Think about a person who has become true spiritual family to you. What are ways you can bless and thank this person for their devotion, love, and encouragement?

_____

_____

_____

_____

_____

How do you respond to people who are deep in sin and far from God? How should Jesus's encounter with the woman at the well influence the way you relate to people who come from the "other side of the tracks" and who are very different than you?

_____

_____

_____

_____

_____

The disciples fell asleep when Jesus asked them to watch and pray. How can you be more attentive to the voice and leading of Jesus? How can you hold on to him tighter in the tough times of life?

_____

_____

_____

_____

_____

Action Ideas

Use one or more of the following ideas or exercises to plug into God's power in the coming days:

Mat Carriers

Empowered people know what it feels like to carry the mat of a person in need. They have strained, served, and lifted friends up when they did not have the energy, strength, or hope they needed. Think of someone you care about who is flat on their back right now. Their situation could be physical, emotional, financial, relational, or spiritual, but they are flat out and need someone to help pick them up.

Who is your friend in need? _____

What is their need? _____

What specific action will you take in the coming hours, days, or weeks to help carry this person to Jesus?

_____

_____

Remember, the paralyzed man who was lowered through the roof was carried by four people. Don't hesitate to invite others to help as you seek to serve this friend.

Now, here is the hard part. If you are flat on your back right now (and maybe no one knows it because you have learned to fake it in front of others), it might be time to let others support and carry you. Would you dare to share your situation with a small group of people who love you and allow them to care for you and carry your mat?

Remember, empowered people know there are times when they carry someone's mat and there are also times (for all of us) when we are on the mat and need to humbly let others care for us!

Hand Exam

Take a look at one of your hands. Ask yourself, who are the people who have taken your hand and offered mentoring, spiritual guidance, and help on your journey of faith? Some of them may have passed away and are now with Jesus. Others still hold your hand and offer regular support along the way.

Take time to thank God for these people and pray for strength and wisdom to receive all God offers you through their lives.

Next, look at your other hand. Think about the people you are helping grow in faith. How is God using you to move them forward in spiritual maturity? What are some ways you can be more active in helping them and encouraging them to climb higher in their journey of following Jesus?

Finally, who is one person you know who needs someone to take their hand and help them along in faith? Prayerfully ask God if there is some role he would have you take in this person's life. If you feel a nudge of the Holy Spirit, take action!

Seeking and Loving the Outcast

Take time to do a deep, honest, rigorous examination of your attitude toward those who are different than you, people who live on the "other side of the tracks," or those who have made poor choices and are living in the consequences of sin. Are there people you avoid? Are there entire groups of people you look down on? Just between you and Jesus, are there some folks you hope don't show up on your doorstep or at your church?

These are people loved by God. They need the grace of Jesus as much as you do. God wants them to be your brothers and sisters in faith. He actually wants you to be part of his mission to reach out and love those who are broken and outcast.

Remember Jesus at the well, having a theological conversation with a Samaritan woman who had been through five husbands and was now living with another man. Let your heart become like your Savior's heart. Pray for God to show you people whom you tend to avoid and make a concerted effort to seek these people out and get to know them. God might just start a revival through someone you dare to reach out to with the love of Jesus!

SECTION 3

Empowered for the Journey by Receiving God's Rest

This is what the Sovereign LORD, the Holy One of Israel, says:

> "In repentance and rest is your salvation,
>   in quietness and trust is your strength,
>   but you would have none of it."

Isaiah 30:15

Come to me, all you who are weary and burdened, and I will give you rest. Take my yoke upon you and learn from me, for I am gentle and humble in heart, and you will find rest for your souls. For my yoke is easy and my burden is light.

Matthew 11:28–30

13

God's Example

Why Would God Take a Day Off?

By the seventh day God had finished the work he had been doing; so on the seventh day he rested from all his work. Then God blessed the seventh day and made it holy, because on it he rested from all the work of creating that he had done.

Genesis 2:2–3

God spoke, created, shaped, and formed the heavens and the earth. With beauty and astounding diversity, he made animals, fish, and birds. As the apex and crown of his creative process, he made a man and a woman. During his creative process, God noticed and declared that the work he had done was good.

Then, God did something shocking and unexpected. The omnipotent and glorious One did something that could seem entirely unnecessary. He took a day off!

God rested.

The almighty, all-powerful, glorious God of heaven took a Sabbath.

The question we must ask is, why? Why did God rest?

117

We know it was *not* because he was tired. God does *not* need to take a nap after a hard day or week of labor. He never has to take a break because of fatigue or emotional stress due to the sheer number of chores he has to check off some heavenly to-do list. God does *not* need to sabbath for his own sake, he does *not* need to rest, and he certainly does *not* need time away to recharge his divine batteries.

He is the eternal source of power. He made and sustains all things. God has more power than an infinite Energizer Bunny. So, why the day off?

I have a theory as to at least one reason God rested on the seventh day. I believe he did it for us. He was setting an example. He was modeling what his children need to do if we are going to stay healthy, whole, and empowered.

Have you ever watched a mother trying to get her baby to eat one of those little jars of baby food? I have. I remember the first time I saw my wife, Sherry, sit with our baby boy Zachariah and try to coax him to eat some puréed meat from a jar. She warmed it up in the microwave and the smell was less than pleasant. She scooped the brownish gray goop onto a little plastic spoon, and then moved it slowly toward his lips making gentle promises of how wonderful it was going to be. "It's gooood! Try it. Come on, Zach, you will like it. It's delicious," she cooed.

He was not buying what she was selling. He turned his face away and his nose up in the air. Then, he pressed his baby lips together as if to say, "There is no way I am eating that gruel."

I don't know if it was the smell, the look, or just an innate sense that this was not going to be as "delicious" as he was being led to believe. But as I watched, it struck me that our little boy was reacting just like I would have if someone tried to put a spoonful of that stuff in my mouth.

He had no idea how good it was for him. He knew nothing about the nutrients and protein packed in that little jar. He was not thinking about his own health and growth. He was simply rejecting something that looked and smelled suspicious.

My wife did something that astounded, amazed, and impressed me. It was something I would never have done. She took the encounter up a notch. Sherry looked our baby boy in the eyes and said, "Zach, watch Mommy."

I found myself looking on and thinking, *No way! She is not going to do it!* Then, before I knew it, she actually did.

Sherry took a scoop of mashed meat, looked at Zach, and slowly inserted the spoon into her own mouth. She ate it, keeping her eyes locked with our son's eyes as she smiled and said, "That is good, soooo gooood!" I found myself thinking, *I don't know how many dads would do that, but I know one that would not . . . me!*

What happened next was even more shocking. Zach opened his mouth to receive a spoonful of this strange tan-colored mush. He ate it!

He trusted his mommy. When he saw what she did, he was in. He was ready to try it.

When I think of God taking a Sabbath and resting, this is the picture that comes to my mind. It is as if our heavenly Father is looking into the eyes of his beloved children and saying, "Look at Daddy, watch Daddy, this is what I want you to do. It is good for you, soooo gooood!" It was an example for the finite children of the infinite God. Like my wife modeled eating baby food, God has shown us what he wants us to do. He knows what is best for us even when we do not. He loves us so much that he will gently model something he does not need but his kids do!

God does not need to rest, sabbath, or take a nap. We need all of these things. How does God teach us the importance of a rhythm of rest in our lives? He showed us. He tenderly looks in our eyes and says, "Hey, buddy . . . here, sweetie . . . this is what I want you to do. Watch Daddy and learn."

Our heavenly Father knows us better than we know ourselves. He made us. He is the Creator and we are his creation. His batteries never run down. His reservoirs of power never run out. Ours do.

One of the ways God calls us to live an empowered life is to punctuate each week with a day of rest and refreshment. This cycle of one in seven is locked into the very creation of the universe. It has been modeled by our heavenly Daddy. It is not just a suggestion but the very desire of God's heart that you and I learn to rest on a weekly basis.

Do you hear God speaking to you? "Watch your Daddy. Look, I am resting. I am taking a day off. I worked hard for six days and made the whole universe by my word and my hands. Now, I will sabbath." Can you see the tender eyes of your Maker locked onto your eyes? Do you see his love for you, his tender care, his plea that you will follow his example of resting?

He did not do it for himself. God rested for us. He knows what is best for his finite children. Are you ready to hear his invitation and follow his example?

The pattern is simple. It is a rhythm of one in seven. Each week, we are given the gift of a day that is very different than all the others. This is not to become a legalistic chore, but to be received and embraced with joy. Jesus was clear that Sabbath was given for us, to refresh and bless. We were not made to be enslaved to a set of human rules and regulations about the Sabbath day.[1]

So what should this day look like? What is it that our Father desires for us? In the most simple terms, it should be a day of rest. We should cease and desist from the things we do the other six days of the week. Instead, we should do that which recharges our batteries, invigorates our soul, and refreshes our bodies. This is not about an inflexible list of dos and don'ts. It is about figuring out what is truly restful for us.

I had a member of my congregation talk with me on a Sunday after I had preached about the gift and importance of a weekly day of rest. She was a highly competent and hardworking person who held a very high elected government office. She worked hard five to six days a week, but Sunday was her island of refreshment. She was faithful in attending worship services as part of her day, but then she loved to putter in her garden on Sunday afternoons. She had grown up being told that "work" was to be avoided on her day of rest. The dilemma was, gardening was not work for her. It was restful and refreshing. She asked if she was doing something wrong by spending her afternoon picking weeds, tending her garden, and getting her hands into the soil.

Had she been a farmer, I would have encouraged her to avoid the garden on her Sabbath day. But she was a politician who found peace, met Jesus, and was refreshed by this activity . . . it was not work for her. I believe that God looked at her as she watered and tended her garden and took delight. This was rest. She was accepting the gift.

If we want to learn the lesson God modeled for us all the way back in the beginning, we need to discover what refreshes us. It could be a nap or a ten-mile run. It might be reading a great book or taking a long drive. A walk on the golf course could refresh some people, but for others this would not be restful at all. I would never try to define what constitutes rest for any other person because we are all wired differently and the content of our week varies dramatically. Instead, we each need to pray and ask God to help us discover the things that really do bring us rest. Then one day a week, we should fully enjoy these things. In the same way, we can identify what depletes and drains us and avoid these things one day a week.[2]

Powerful people turn their head away and their nose up. They are not opening their mouth and partaking of the whole Sabbath rest program. They believe they can press on seven days a week and that their reserve will never run dry.

Powerless people don't know what a full workweek looks like. They don't need to take a nap but they should get up and work harder. They like the idea of rest so much that they have turned it into an art form.

Empowered people discover the beautiful and health-giving rhythm of life that flows from hard and vigorous work to refreshing rest and play. They hear the voice of their heavenly Father calling them to open wide and receive his gift of rest. As they receive heavenly refreshment through weekly Sabbath and daily time in God's presence, they feel their spiritual, physical, and emotional batteries charge up. They are ready for a new week of serving, working, living, and loving for Jesus.

From the Heart of the Father

My Child,

Embrace the gift of rest. Don't run so hard that you collapse. You were not made for ceaseless work. Embrace your vocation as a gift, but don't let it consume your life, your heart, your relationships, or your body.

There is a rhythm programmed into your body and soul. Each week, take a day to rest, be refreshed, play, and even take a nap. The universe will continue on without your help, it really will! Just unplug, be filled, and enjoy the Sabbath rest you so deeply need.

▸▸ **Walk with God** and learn more about how you can experience the strength of Sabbath rest by reading Genesis 1–2.

14

Moses's Teaching

Called to Rest

Remember the Sabbath day by keeping it holy. Six days you shall labor and do all your work, but the seventh day is a sabbath to the LORD your God. On it you shall not do any work, neither you, nor your son or daughter, nor your male or female servant, nor your animals, nor any foreigner residing in your towns. For in six days the LORD made the heavens and the earth, the sea, and all that is in them, but he rested on the seventh day. Therefore the LORD blessed the Sabbath day and made it holy.

Exodus 20:8–11

Egypt and the Red Sea were behind them. The people of Israel were dining on manna and quail and a whole new future was before them. After four hundred years in Egypt, they were finally moving toward the promise given through Abraham centuries earlier.[1] They had come to Mount Sinai. They were on the edge of the Promised Land.

God spoke through his servant Moses and told the people that they must always remember how he had delivered them on eagles' wings and brought them out of slavery. God promised his chosen

123

people that if they fully keep the covenant, they would be his "treasured possession," "a kingdom of priests," and "a holy nation."[2]

The people of God watched as the Lord descended on the mountain in fire and smoke. They felt the mountain quake beneath their feet. God was with them. Moses was called up the mountain to meet with Yahweh.[3] This was to become one of the high points in the history of God's people and the world! God was going to give the Law . . . the Ten Commandments. These would be clear declarations of God's will for those who follow him. The One who made the universe would clarify how people are to walk with him and each other.

What would you expect God to say? What commandments would make the most sense as God was forming a new nation and a new movement that would change the trajectory of the human family?

Honor God above everything and everyone. That makes sense.

No idols or images. In a time of history where most families had their own wood, stone, or metal idols that they bowed down to worship as gods, this would be essential. They were entering a land that was riddled with idols and littered with false places of worship; clarity about idolatry was a must.

Don't murder. This makes sense in every generation and location.

Don't steal. We can all nod our heads to affirm this one.

Don't commit adultery. Amen!

As we read the commandments given to Moses and inscribed on the tables of stone, they make sense. These are things on which you can build a culture, a family, and a people of faith. But, there is one of the Ten Commandments that seems strange and out of place, at first glance.

Brace yourself.

Here it is.

In a spiritual nutshell the fourth commandment is . . . *Be sure to rest. Take a Sabbath. Every seven days, unplug, relax, cease work, and get refreshed.*

How does that fit in with "No idols" and "Don't murder"? At first blush, the call to "Remember the Sabbath day by keeping it holy" seems strangely out of place. It looks like a 95-pound junior high school lineman on a football field facing a 310-pound professional.

Yet as we read Exodus and the rest of the Bible, we hear God call his people to take a Sabbath rest. It was for them, those who worked for them, and even their animals. To top it off, we are reminded that this command is rooted in the very fabric of the universe's creation. Then, to ice the cake, we are reminded that God himself rested on the seventh day.[4] What is going on here? What is so important about the Sabbath that it made God's ultimate Top Ten List?

I was sitting outside a café on a warm summer day when a pastor friend of mine drove up and walked over to meet me for a beverage and some time to talk, pray, and get caught up. As he flopped into the chair across from me, he sighed and said, "I have not taken a day off in three weeks!" His comment did not feel like an arrogant declaration of how hard he was working. It was just an honest acknowledgment of a schedule that had spun out of control.

My response surprised both him and me.

"That's sin!" I barked out with deep conviction.

He looked hurt and shocked at the same time.

We had been friends for many years and had always been very honest with each other. We have one of those incredibly valuable "iron sharpens iron" friendships.[5] So I continued and said something like, "I would be just as concerned for you if you had sat down and said, 'I have been having an affair for the past three weeks,' or 'I murdered someone.'"

We stared at each other for a moment and then launched into a serious conversation about the fact that the Ten Commandments call us to not murder, not commit adultery, and not misuse God's name. Both of us agreed that we believe God was serious about these commandments for the ancient world. We also both believed that these commandments still speak to us today. But we also admitted that the command given through Moses to keep a weekly rhythm of rest called Sabbath can easily be brushed aside.

My friend agreed that he would never have sat with me and tried to rationalize killing a congregational member or having an affair. He would not have plopped down in the chair across from me and tossed out, in a cavalier tone, "I just stole $5,000 from my church's offering." But it did not even faze him to proclaim, "I am a Sabbath breaker!"

We debated. We argued a bit. We talked about what the Bible teaches us about this topic. We grappled with what it means to "Remember the Sabbath day by keeping it holy" in our day and age. And at the end of the conversation, we both felt a clear and strong conviction from the Holy Spirit that we needed to learn how to embrace and appreciate the gift of rest at a whole new level.

We each repented of how easily we can set aside this command and become so engaged in our work that we forget that our heavenly Father has called us to rest one day out of seven each week.

Since that day, more than a decade ago, I have tried to follow the teaching of God given through Moses on Mount Sinai thousands of years ago. I have grown to see Sabbath as a good gift. God has taught me that he knows me better than I know myself and he says I need a rhythm of rest so that I can live for him and serve him over the long haul. I have decided that God is way smarter than me and I am learning to take delight in the gift of rest, even when I think I don't need it.

One thing I have learned is that the exact day of the week is not the primary issue when it comes to honoring God by embracing Sabbath. The ancient Jews, and some today, observed their Sabbath from sundown on Friday to sundown on Saturday. Many Christians who seek to keep this weekly rhythm set Sunday aside for worship, connecting with loved ones, and resting. For me, neither of these work. As a pastor, my weekends are a blitz of multiple church services, many responsibilities, and very little margin. But Thursday has become a day of delight in my life. I look forward to it, I guard it, I love it! On this day, I do the things that fill me and refresh me . . . I sabbath.

Along with doing the things we find restful on our Sabbath, another way to fully embrace the gift of this day is to connect with

God and people. Jesus was clear that the most important of all the commandments is to love God with everything we have, and to love people.[6] Our Sabbath should reflect the spirit of this Great Commandment! On this day, make space for God. If you sabbath on a day when you can attend a corporate worship service, make this part of the flow of your day. Don't just go to church, but meet with God, worship, seek his face, celebrate his grace. If, like me, there is not a worship service available to you on your Sabbath day, set aside a good portion of time to sit at the feet of Jesus, feed on his Word, talk with him in prayer, sing to him, and rest in the presence of the One who can fill you up for the coming week and empower you for the challenges that lie ahead.

In addition, connect with people on your Sabbath day. It might be helpful for you to have some time to pull away and withdraw from others. But also remember that Jesus called you to love your neighbor as yourself. A Sabbath day can be a perfect time to linger with a family member to get caught up, listen to their stories, and pray with them. It can be a time to call a friend who has fallen a bit off the map and reconnect with them. This could be a time to make space for friends and people in your life who are far from God. During our workweek we can run hard and fast. Sometimes we end up rushing past those who matter most. On our Sabbath day we can slow down and focus on the gift of the people God has graciously placed in our life.

Powerful people hear the call of God to rest and take a Sabbath every week, but they cleverly design ways to convince themselves that this rhythm of a rested life is not necessary for them.

The powerless know how to rest. They don't have to worry about taking a day off; they have orchestrated a life where others do most of the work because they feel incapable of carrying much of a load.

Empowered men and women are discovering the joy-filled journey of working hard and resting well. These people love their labor and see it as a gift from God. They work hard and take delight in being productive. At the same time, they know how to shut down, walk away, and rest well. They can play hard and work hard.

Each time they embrace the gift of Sabbath, these people are empowered to live another week for the glory of God. Their time with God and people actually fuels their work and makes them more productive. They have discovered that the God who made them actually knows their needs better than they do. With time, Sabbath becomes an act of worship, a gift they appreciate, and a health-giving rhythm of life.

From the Heart of Moses

Faint and Weary Friend,

Listen to God. He made you. He loves you. He knows what you need.

He has offered a gift, one that you long for even if you don't know it. Your need for regular rest is so essential to your spiritual, emotional, and physical health that your Maker does more than suggest you take a weekly Sabbath. He commands it!

Right up there with "Don't murder" and "Don't steal" is "Be sure to rest." It is so important that God wrote it in stone with his own finger.

Stop resisting God's call to a rested life. Embrace a new lifestyle of resting one day out of seven each week. Call your friends and family to do the same.

Step away, breathe deep, take a nap, sing songs of praise to God, sit in silence, read the Scriptures, play, enjoy friends, and drink in the goodness of God's creation. You were made for more than grinding out day after day after endless day of work. You can find God's power as you learn to rest.

▸▸ **Walk with Moses** and learn more about how you can experience the strength of Sabbath rest by reading Exodus 20 and Deuteronomy 5.

15

Israel's Struggle

Resistance, Manna, and Maggots

The Israelites did as they were told; some gathered much, some little. And when they measured it by the omer, the one who gathered much did not have too much, and the one who gathered little did not have too little. Everyone had gathered just as much as they needed. Then Moses said to them, "No one is to keep any of it until morning." However, some of them paid no attention to Moses; they kept part of it until morning, but it was full of maggots and began to smell. So Moses was angry with them.

Exodus 16:17–20

The people of Israel were hungry. Not the hunger that comes when it has been a couple of hours since your third meal of the day and you just have to microwave some popcorn. That is not real hunger. God's people were facing a situation that could lead to hunger that would kill them. They were in a desert with a limited and dwindling food supply and a massive number of mouths to feed.

In desperate times we have many options for how we will respond. Two of the most popular responses among the people of

Israel were seeking God through passionate prayer *or* complaining to God by grumbling about their circumstances. In this case they went for option number two. They whined, complained, and grumbled.[1]

In grace, God answered and provided all the people needed. He gave meat in the evening and bread in the morning. God heard their complaints and answered with grace and abundance![2]

It was the responsibility of Moses to lead the people during their wandering through the desert. He gave God's instructions to the nation of Israel so they would know how to gather and consume the heavenly breakfast God provided day after day. If Moses had a quarter for every time the people of Israel ignored his instructions, grumbled about his leadership, or rebelled against what he called them to do, he would have been unthinkably rich! It seemed that the knee-jerk response to any of Moses's instructions was to do the opposite. They were flat-out stubborn and rebellious.

In Exodus 16 we read a story about God's people ignoring the leadership of Moses. The sad reality is that the instructions were not from Moses but from God.

The Maker of heaven had heard the voice of his people and had poured down manna from above. It was heavenly cereal that tasted as sweet as honey. They had never seen anything like it before, so they named it "what is it," or *manna*. You would think at this point in their journey the nation of Israel would have written a collective thank-you note to God and Moses for putting up with their incessant whining and rebellion.

Instead, they refused to follow the simple and clear instructions for manna collection and consumption. God was crystal clear: instruction number one . . . go out each morning and gather just as much as each person needs for the day, an omer of manna each. Instruction number two . . . eat your manna. Instruction three . . . don't keep any manna until the morning. Eat the day's allotment that day.

This was not a fifteen-step, complex set of instructions. Just pick up what you need and eat it that day. No hoarding or saving. No manna storage or stockpiling. Trust God to provide what you need for each day.

Some of the people decided they had a better plan. They kept their manna until the morning. This was a sign, a simple indicator of the condition of their hearts and the shallowness of their faith. Their manna-hoarding behavior screamed, "I don't trust God to provide for tomorrow." The result was profound. The next morning, when they opened up their secret stockpile of manna . . . Surprise! It was rotten.[3]

Have you ever seen a dead animal on the side of the road, all bloated, decomposing, riddled with maggots, and stinking to high heaven? That was the condition of day-old manna. Just one night of storage and the heavenly sweet cereal became utterly grotesque.

There is no doubt that the talk around the camp of Israel was, "Don't save manna overnight! If you do, your house will stink in the morning and you will have to spend the day cleaning out the maggots." Once the word got around the camp, no one was going to gather extra manna and leave it on the kitchen counter until the next day.

Imagine the response to Moses when he came to the people and instructed them to gather a double portion of manna on Friday so they could save some to eat on Saturday. The people were not good at following Moses's instructions when they were simple and reasonable. Now he was calling them to do something they had already learned would lead to maggots and a horrible smell in their home.

By God's leading, Moses told the people they were not to go out and collect manna on the Sabbath day; this was a day of rest. This led to one new instruction. Collect double manna on day six and store it overnight so that they would have nourishment on the Sabbath.[4]

Picture these grumbling, whining, rebellious people opening their container of manna on the Sabbath day after it had sat for the night. Can you see them plugging their nose, averting their eyes, not wanting to smell the stench or see the maggots crawling through their manna? Have you ever opened a mystery container that has been forgotten in the corner of your refrigerator for weeks or months? You know the feeling of being reluctant to look at whatever science experiment has been growing in your refrigerator? If you have had this experience, you have a sense of what they must have felt as they opened their manna container.

To their shock, the manna was fresh and sweet. No heinous smell. No crawling bugs. Just heavenly breakfast.

The laws of nature were altered. It was a culinary miracle. The heavenly bread that fell on the earth six days of the week did not appear on the Sabbath. The same substance that rotted overnight and became a breeding ground for maggots when collected the other days of the week was perfectly fresh on the Sabbath.

What is God teaching his people? What lessons echo through history to God's children today? Try these on for size. God can provide for all of our needs in six days of labor and life. Faithful people can embrace a day of rest each week and trust God to take care of them and the universe. Rest is a gift and God is very serious about our learning a rhythm of life that makes space for six days of labor and one of Sabbath.

The powerful have a way of getting things done, and it is always their way. God gives clear direction and calls them to a natural flow of work punctuated by rest, but they have a better idea. When God says, "Sabbath," they have a unique capacity to rationalize and explain why they should collect manna seven days a week.

The powerless have a different flow of life. They don't struggle with embracing the invitation to rest. The problem is that they don't think they have what it takes to gather their own manna. They want someone else to gather and provide what they need. Rest is for those who have worked hard the other days of the week, and the powerless have not broken a sweat or put their shoulder to plow.

Empowered people have discovered that God has an endless supply of all we need. They have learned that God has given work as a good gift and they go out to gather manna for themselves and those they love. They are thankful for the blessing of meaningful labor. At the same time, they have embraced the gift of Sabbath rest. They know that God is able to provide all they need in six days of labor so they faithfully walk away from work one day a week. This rhythm of rest fills them with energy, vision, and a fresh spirit to work hard for the glory of God the next week, and the one after that.

From the Heart of God's Wandering People

Dear Brothers and Sisters,

Don't fight God's wisdom. He made the universe and he created you. He really does know best. When he calls us to work and gather only six days and rest one day a week, he means it. Don't choose to resist God and learn the hard way. Unless you really like bad smells and maggots!

Accept God's gracious gift of rest. Trust his ability to provide for you in only six days of work, labor, and gathering. Believe that God delights to provide what you need, as only a loving Father can. Then, take a day to cease from your work, find rest in God, be with people you love, worship the One who loves you, and drink in his refreshment.

God is on the throne and he can provide everything you need and more. Declare your trust and faith in him by learning to rest and sabbath well. When you do, you will open your jar of manna after it has sat overnight and discover it is fresh, sweet, and there is enough to fill you to overflowing!

▸▸ **Walk with God's People** and learn more about how you can experience the strength of Sabbath rest by reading Exodus 16 and Numbers 11.

16

David's Shepherd Psalm

Green Pastures and Still Waters

The LORD is my shepherd, I lack nothing.
   He makes me lie down in green pastures,
he leads me beside quiet waters,
   he refreshes my soul.

Psalm 23:1–3

He was the youngest of seven sons. In the ancient world, as in our world, the youngest was often tasked with the worst of the household chores and least desired of the jobs in the family business. This is why David took care of the sheep, the family flock. He learned the trade. His job: graze the sheep, keep them full, and whatever you do, don't lose one. Bring them all home alive.

In modern days we can romanticize the role of a shepherd. Lush green pastures, quiet nights, strumming a small harp and singing songs to God while the sheep rested. The truth is, it was a hard, thankless, isolated job. It was also dangerous.

There were many reasons shepherds became experts with a sling and stone. Three of them were thieves, lions, and bears. Hand-to-hand combat was not unheard of, and David had battled to protect his flock on many occasions. A lion had pounced from the thicket, latched his teeth on one of David's sheep, and carried it off. David tracked it down, pounced on the lion, grabbed its thick coat, and beat the beast to death. The shepherd boy had a similar encounter with a bear, and when it was over, the beast was dead and David carried the mauled sheep back to his flock. Let's just say that David took his job seriously![1]

What do you do when you have countless hours alone with sheep? You practice flinging stones until you can send them flying with laserlike accuracy and bone-crushing velocity. You never know when a wild animal, thief, or giant might come your way. You scour the horizon for any threat to your flock. You look for safe and lush pastures and fresh water to nourish your sheep. And as you walk the meadows and mountainsides, you watch, study, and learn more about sheep than you dreamed anyone could know. You also learn about yourself. As a shepherd you discover what it means to provide, protect, and lead a flock.

Through his childhood, David gained a clear sense of the role of a shepherd and the place of the sheep. At some point the shepherd boy began to make a comparison, a spiritual connection that became a Holy Spirit–inspired song. David realized that God is the Shepherd, his Shepherd. Just as important, he realized in the core of his being that he was a sheep of God's pasture.

Somehow, in his young soul, something took root. David, the lion-killing, bear-defeating child warrior, realized that God loved him more than David loved his sheep. He was ready to die for his flock . . . and almost did on a number of occasions. Could it be that God loved him, protected him, attentively watched over him, and provided for him just like a loving shepherd?

This is what David learned about his Shepherd-God after thousands of hours watching the family flock and seeking to be the best shepherd he could be:

- He is my *shepherd*,
- He makes me *lie down* (in lush pasturelands),

- He *leads* me (to still and refreshing waters),
- He *refreshes* my soul,
- He *guides* me (along the right paths . . . for the glory of his name),
- He is *present* with me,
- He *protects and comforts* me (with his rod and staff),
- He *prepares* a table for me (right in the presence of my enemies),
- He *anoints* my head with oil,
- He *fills* my cup to overflowing, and
- He *pursues* me with goodness and love (my whole life).

Just take a deep breath and draw these truths into your lungs and soul. You might want to read them one more time. The Good Shepherd who loves you is ready to do all of this for you, the sheep of his pasture. When a man, woman, or young person places their faith in Jesus, the Lord becomes their Shepherd and wants to lead them to restful places of refreshment, safety, and comfort. As their Shepherd, he is ready to protect them to the point of death!

Another way God watches over his flock is to empower them by leading his sheep to times, places, and seasons of deep rest and refreshment. We are not called to retreat from the world and hide in a cave or church building. We are still in the world as God's salt and light. But when we walk with the Good Shepherd, we are assured that there is guidance, anointing, and overflow from his endless supply. We experience his strong comfort, a hand of protection and discipline that empowers us and fills us with confidence in God.

What peace flows into the heart of a sheep that knows the Good Shepherd has their best interests in mind. What deep sleep and rest falls on a person who looks up and sees their Shepherd on the watch, sling and stone ready, eyes fixed on the horizon looking for any threat or enemy. What confidence fills the heart of a Jesus-following sheep when we know that the Savior has already fought the battle with our worst enemy and won the victory! We have been rescued from the teeth and claws of the prowling lion and carried safely back to the flock of the Father.[2]

David's shepherd song helps ordinary sheep understand who they are and their relationship with God:

- I lack nothing,
- I *fearlessly walk* through the dark valley,
- I am *pursued by goodness* and love (every day of my life),
- I dwell in God's house forever!

Chew on these truths like a sheep and let them digest slowly. As you read Psalm 23, this favorite and famous chapter of Scripture, take note of who you are: a full, fearless, forever child of God, pursued by his goodness and love.

Looking for a source of daily empowerment? Let these truths fill your heart and mind just as they saturated the soul of the young shepherd David thousands of years ago. Picture yourself tending sheep on a lonely hillside. Imagine that you had battled lions, bears, and thieves. What might it feel like to risk your life for the flock? Try to envision yourself spending countless hours looking for fresh grass, green pastures for the flock, clean water, and a safe place to bed them down for the night.

What might you learn from David's heart and the Word of God?

- I am his loved sheep,
- I *lie down* in green pastures near fresh water,
- My soul can be *refreshed* each day,
- I am *guided* so my life can bring him glory,
- I am *never alone*, even in the very hard times,
- I am *protected* by the very hand of God,
- I am *provided for* even when persecution arises,
- I am *anointed* by God, and
- I am given a *surplus*.

Near our home in Monterey are many miles of open and rolling hills. My wife Sherry and I go hiking in these hills almost every Saturday morning. At certain times of the year, there is a flock of about four hundred sheep that wander the hills, bleat loudly, and eat the grass. There is also a shepherd who watches over them with attentive eyes. I have been told that the county pays for this service because it is the best way to keep the natural grasses from growing too tall and becoming a fire hazard. I have also been told there are mountain lions in the hills near our home. I know this is true because one morning, as the sun was rising, I saw one. Even modern-day shepherds in Monterey have to be ready to fight for their flock.

Sherry and I have studied these sheep. We have seen them up close. One time, as we were hiking, the flock was crossing right in front of us. We just kept walking and they parted like the Red Sea as we walked near. We hiked for a short time with sheep 360 degrees around us. Because of these encounters, the lessons of Psalm 23 have been reinforced in my mind and heart.

Sheep seem quite vulnerable. They have no fangs and no claws, and they don't strike me as fighters. The shepherd is always watching. One day, as we were hiking among the sheep in the Toro Hills, I studied the shepherd who was nearby watching over his flock. I tried to count how many seconds he would turn his back on the flock or look away. I never got past four. Even when the shepherd was walking up a hill with his back to the flock, every three to four seconds he turned his head and observed his flock grazing on the adjoining hills. Also, when a sheep would wander too far from the flock, he would whistle and his three dogs would take off full-speed and move the stray right back with the other sheep. It was beautiful in its simplicity. When the sheep are in the hills near our home, the shepherd is always present, protecting, providing water, keeping them together, and watching.

In the Old Testament David declares that the Lord is our Shepherd and we are his sheep. In the New Testament Jesus calls himself the Good Shepherd and assures us that he will lay his life down for his flock. He knows each of us personally and we recognize his voice when he speaks to us.[3] We can rest and be at peace because our Shepherd is near, always watching, providing, and protecting.

The powerful seek to provide all they need for themselves, protect themselves and those they love, and walk as if they are fearless in their own strength. They believe they need no Shepherd because they see themselves as strong and able to take care of themselves.

The powerless look to God as their provider, protector, and leader and expect him to take care of everything for them. Their job is to lie by still waters in green pastures and let God take care of the universe, the world, their family, and them. "Hey, I'm a sheep, what can I do!"

The *empowered* draw from the amazing reserve and abundance of their Shepherd and rejoice in this provision. But they also realize that God fills them, leads them, and provides for them. Empowered people are not retreating from the world when they rest, they are getting charged up for another day following the Shepherd. Empowered Christians love the quiet times of still water and green pastures. They also know that the same God who leads them to times of rest and refreshment calls them to invite those who are still lost sheep to join them in the presence of the Good Shepherd. Still waters, green pastures, and the presence of a loving Shepherd are not just for us. These are to be shared.

From the Heart of David, a Sheep of God's Pasture

Fellow Sheep,

Look up on the hillside. Do you see your Shepherd? Trust him. Follow him. Know that he would fight for you, protect you at all costs, and die for you!

When he leads you to quiet waters, drink deeply. When he brings you to green pastures, eat, rest, and know you are safe. Your well-being does not come because there are no threats or enemies. There are lions and bears in the hills, there always have been. But your Shepherd is watching, ever ready to spring into action on your behalf.

Once you are well-fed, rested, and refreshed, get up and follow the Shepherd. That is your most important duty. Don't wander away. Don't choose your own path. Keep your eyes on the Shepherd and your ears open to his voice.

Follow. Just follow, and you will never be lost.

▶▶ **Walk with David** and learn more about how you can find rest under the care of the Good Shepherd by reading Psalm 23; 1 Samuel 17; and John 10.

17

Elijah's Turning Point

The Value of a Nap and a Snack

> Then he lay down under the bush and fell asleep. All at once an angel touched him and said, "Get up and eat." He looked around, and there by his head was some bread baked over hot coals, and a jar of water. He ate and drank and then lay down again.
>
> 1 Kings 19:5–6

Sometimes life's low points seem to come tagging along on the heels of our best and most triumphant moments. What is true for you and me was also true for many of the Bible's most faithful people.

Elijah had just joined hands and hearts with God to face what seemed to be impossible odds. It was not one against ten, or one versus one hundred. The spiritual brawl Elijah had entered, with God as his tag team partner, was one true prophet against 850 false prophets. Of course God was on Elijah's side, but the scene on top of Mount Carmel, where this battle royal would take place, must have looked like a laughably uneven playing field.

On one side of the mount, 450 prophets of Baal, the god of weather, storm, and fertility. He was a very popular deity among

141

the locals. Partnered with these false prophets were 400 prophets of Asherah, the she-goddess and mistress of Baal. Get the picture? Can you see it in your mind? Eight hundred fifty false prophets dressed in their official prophetic garb and fiercely antagonistic toward Elijah and Yahweh.

On the other side of Mount Carmel stood Elijah. To the human observer, alone. So very alone.

You can read all about this spiritual slugfest in 1 Kings 18, but when the final round was completed, the prophets of Baal and Asherah were dead, Elijah was still standing, and the God of Israel was lifted up as glorious and victorious.

If there was ever a time in Elijah's prophetic life of ministry where he could have felt powerful and ready to stand on his own, this would have been the moment. The smell of the sacrifice he had offered was still in the air and the smoke of the fire that his God had hurled from heaven was billowing upward. The people had repented and cried out, "The Lord, he is God!" The celebration party was in full swing! Elijah was at the top of his game, his stock was skyrocketing, and everyone knew it.

Right in the middle of this meteoric moment of Elijah's influence and success, he received a message from Queen Jezebel. It was no more than a brief postcard with only one sentence. Jezebel declared to the prophet Elijah, "May the gods deal with me, be it ever so severely, if by this time tomorrow I do not make your life like that of one of them."[1]

Translation: "You just had my 850 prophets killed. You are next!"

How would Elijah respond? How would this true prophet of God react to the threat of one woman who had bowed her knees to false gods and rebelled against Yahweh? He had just seen God send fire from heaven, he had just watched Jezebel's mighty host of prophets fail in the battle and fall under the sword. He had never been more popular with the people.

Watch closely and take note of the attitude and actions of Elijah: "Elijah was afraid and ran for his life."[2]

For some reason, Elijah was not feeling powerful. He saw himself as powerless. The threat of one woman sent spiritual shivers down his prophetic spine and he was overcome with terror. The same man who had just stood face-to-face and toe-to-toe with 850 false prophets and had seen God bring a miraculous victory was now running from one reprobate queen.

It got worse. When he ran far enough that he felt he was out of harm's way, at least for the moment, Elijah flopped down and had a talk with God. His words are surprising and heart wrenching. Elijah told God three things:

I have had enough!

I want to die!

My life is worthless![3]

Are these the words and prayers of a powerful man? Do you see confidence and boldness at this moment in Elijah's life? What was going on here?

Elijah was feeling powerless, paralyzed by fear, and hopeless. In this state of mind, Elijah fell asleep . . . exhausted!

What did the prophet need at this moment? Did he need to increase his self-esteem, read a book on positive confession, or attend a seminar on embracing his inner prophet's power? No, no, and definitely no!

What he needed was a nap, a snack, and the gentle touch of the God who loved him. He needed an infilling of grace, care, and strength from the hand of his Lord.

After a time of napping, God sent an angel to wake Elijah up with a simple and almost humorous directive, "Get up and eat." Have a snack. That was exactly what Elijah needed. After snack time, the weary prophet took another nap.[4]

When the second rest time was over, the angel showed up again and brought him another snack. His message was exactly the same, with one very important addition. "Get up and eat," was repeated. But in addition the angel said, "For the journey is too much for you."[5]

What comforting words! What a beautiful account!

God let Elijah rest, he brought him a snack, and then God did it again. There is such tenderness in this account. Like a loving mother with a weary child encourages a nap and a little sustenance, God cared for his fear-filled and exhausted child. Then Elijah was reminded of what he already knew so deeply and personally: "The journey is too much for you."

God wanted his little boy, the mighty prophet, to know that what lay ahead was too much for him to do alone. It was over his head, out of his reach, and impossible for Elijah to accomplish . . . in his own strength.

The point should be clear by now. Elijah was not powerful and able to fulfill the call and mission of God in his own abilities, creativity, or strength. He was also not powerless and consigned to the desert of Beersheba where he would sleep until he died. Elijah was to live an empowered life. He was called to draw on the source of all strength and run with the wind of God's Spirit lifting him.

At that particular moment of Elijah's life, ministry, and journey, he did not need to try harder or be challenged to be stronger. What the great Elijah needed after the battle with the 850 false prophets and the fearful news that the king's wife was gunning for his life was much more basic. Elijah needed a nap and a snack! Then another nap and another snack. After that, he was ready for his next assignment.

After being discouraged and fearful, after a time of rest, after eating what God had placed before him, Elijah got up and traveled for forty days and forty nights. He pressed on until he reached the mountain of God. All was not resolved and God was still going to speak to Elijah and fill him more, but the strength Elijah needed for the next part of his journey was administered to him through God-directed rest.

What do you do when you feel spent, exhausted, under attack, and ready to throw in the towel?

The powerful seek to press on. They dig even deeper into their own personal reserve of strength and try to muster power for one more day, one more battle, one more personal victory. They grit their teeth and press on, believing that they have what it takes to climb the next hill and win the next battle.

The powerless curl up under a broom tree, fall asleep, and refuse to get up again. They are sure they have nothing left to give, no more strength to offer, and no hope of any victory in the future.

The *empowered* look to God for rest. They are comfortable taking a nap, having a snack, and telling God how they really feel. They are honest and transparent. They know that their strength is never enough, but they also know their God has power to spare. They put their trust in the God who watches over them during naptime like a loving and protective parent. They are confident that when exhaustion descends, God will show up with warm bread to fill their belly and cool water to refresh their soul.

The empowered know that after deep rest and a good snack, they will be ready to press on and serve God with renewed passion.

From the Heart of Elijah

Weary One,

You have run hard, worked diligently, and served faithfully. You have pressed on and followed God through the battles and the furnace of this life. Now you are tired. You are weary. You are poured out and empty.

Just stop. Stop working, stop striving, stop pushing, and stop driving forward.

It is time to rest. Open your heart to receive the grace of God and the filling of his Spirit. Open your mouth to eat warm bread and drink cool, fresh water. Take a nap. Put your frazzled and weary mind to bed. Drink in the refreshment of God.

There will be another day to labor for the Lord. He will infuse you and use you again!

But today, rest. Have a snack. Take a nap. Fall exhausted into the arms of God and let him hold you and speak words of comfort, hope, and grace.

▸▸ **Walk with Elijah** and learn more about how you can experience the strength of rest by reading 1 Kings 17:1–19:18.

18

Jesus's Early Mornings

Intimacy with the Father

Very early in the morning, while it was still dark, Jesus got up, left the house and went off to a solitary place, where he prayed.

Mark 1:35

What would it have been like to follow Jesus around for a whole day? We rarely get a glimpse of an entire day in the life of the Savior, but in the Gospel of Mark we get very close.[1] Here is a thumbnail sketch.

We begin in Capernaum. It is the Sabbath day and God's people are gathered to hear the Scriptures and worship. Jesus expounded the Word of God. He taught those who were gathered. He spoke with authority and power that shocked and amazed them. Not even the highly trained and revered teachers of the law spoke with such pure authority.

Right in the middle of Jesus's message, a demon-possessed man cried out and confronted the Savior. Jesus silenced the demon and set the tormented man free. The people were already amazed by

Jesus's authoritative preaching, but his ability to make the demons of hell run for the hills brought their wonder to a whole new level!

You can imagine that Jesus was exhausted after a morning of preaching and ministry (remember, he was fully human), but his day was just getting started. In the afternoon Jesus and his followers gathered at the home of Simon Peter and his brother Andrew. Don't imagine this as a quiet afternoon sharing a meal and telling ministry stories. Simon's mother-in-law was sick, so Jesus shifted back into ministry mode and cared for her. He healed her and got her back on her feet. When the Lord saw a real need, he loved to meet it. On this day, the needs kept rolling in.

Maybe the evening would yield an opportunity for Jesus and his disciples to take a deep breath and slow down for some refreshment.

Not this night.

As the sun went down, the whole town descended on the home where Jesus and his followers were gathered. Sick people came in search of healing. Those tormented by demons made their way in hope of deliverance. Hurting and broken people arrived with a dream that wholeness might be found in the presence, touch, and words of Jesus. A tsunami of human needs and pain came crashing down on the home of Peter and Andrew. The night became a spontaneous service of healing and deliverance. With love and compassion, Jesus ministered to person after person. Broken bodies were healed. Captured souls were set free. Lives were changed for eternity. It was an amazing and long evening of ministry.

What happened next should speak to every faithful follower of Jesus who seeks to spend their days serving God and honoring him. Very early the next day, before the sun came up, Jesus snuck away from the house and went to find a quiet and private place to meet with his Father. Jesus knew the crowds would be gathered soon, looking for him to minister, heal, teach, and set people free. There were many others who wanted the power that only Jesus could bring.

Before Jesus began another full and intense day of ministry, he needed to slip away from the crowds and his friends and be in the presence of his Father. We must always remember that although

Jesus was God, he also had the physical needs and limitations of a man. He grew weary, he became hungry, he thirsted, and he needed rest and refreshment.

Is it appropriate to say that Jesus needed to recharge his batteries and connect with the Father? I believe it is.

Jesus took a mini spiritual retreat. He slipped away to have some quiet time with his Father. This was a time to recalibrate, be refreshed, and recharge.

If Jesus Christ, God in human flesh, needed to find a quiet place where he would not be interrupted as he spent time with the Father, how much more do we need to develop this kind of flow and rhythm in our life? If we are seeking to be like Jesus, then secret moments with the Father will become precious and frequent.

When I became a follower of Jesus in my teenage years, I was given a Bible and told that I was supposed to read it every day and do what it said. I was also encouraged to pray and talk with God about whatever was on my heart. As a bonus, I was told that writing down my prayers in a journal would be a good idea. So I got a journal and spent time every day reading the Bible and writing down some prayers. This was a great discipline and became a habit in my spiritual life.

At one point along the way it struck me that my daily time with God was turning into an item on my daily checklist. It was no longer a passion of my heart. I was meeting with God, in a sense. But mostly I was doing a spiritual chore.

I began evaluating what was driving me and how I spent this "quiet time" with God. I wanted to have a heart like Jesus. I longed to find rest in the arms of the Father after busy days and before a new time of serving him. As the years passed this daily mini-retreat became more organic, fluid, and natural. I looked forward to it. I did not just write out some prayers, I began talking to my heavenly Father and listening for the still small voice of his Holy Spirit. These refreshing times punctuated my life and created a connection with God that fed my soul.

As I would read the Bible, I learned to listen for God's whispers through the pages of the Scriptures, and I heard him speak to me.

I think, over time, my daily retreat from the busyness of life and ministry became a healthy time to meet with God, slow down, and let the truth of Scripture and the leading of the Spirit set the direction of my day.[2]

I also discovered that this time could be in the morning, over the lunch hour, in the evening, or any time I needed a respite and refreshment. It also struck me that I could do this more than once a day. When things became intense, I could sneak away for another brief time with the Father. Rather than being a chore to check off my list, this secret time away with God has become a treasured part of my day and a key to intimacy with my heavenly Father.

These short spiritual retreats take many shapes and forms. For me, the first thing in the morning seems to work because I connect with God better before I turn on my computer, check my phone, and the stuff of life starts flying at me. There are also times when I leave my office and simply take a walk around the church campus where I serve. I quiet myself, pray, reflect, and meet with God.

Just like it happened to Jesus, on these occasional walks people sometimes find me and call me back in to help meet a need. Sometimes I respond and jump in. At other times, like Jesus did, I say that there is other ministry that must happen.[3] On occasion, that ministry is what God needs to do in me before I am ready to head out and care more for people.

Some years ago I invited Juan Carlos Ortiz to speak at a pastors' gathering I convened each year in Michigan. Juan Carlos had pastored a massive church in Argentina and understood the high demands of a busy schedule and life. He had authored a classic book on discipleship and had traveled the world training leaders and preaching the gospel.[4]

What fascinated me about this man was that he spoke to the pastors primarily about meeting with Jesus. Finding a quiet place to sit at the feet of the Savior. He did not bring a lot of teaching about ministry strategy and church growth techniques. His consuming passion was getting these zealous young leaders to love Jesus enough to get away from all the demands and expectations and simply be in the presence of God. He had this idea that all the power we needed for the rough road of ministry could be found in these quiet times of intimacy.

On five or six occasions during the three-day leadership event, Juan Carlos spoke of his secret place where he retreated to meet with his Lord. He described a beautiful brook in a valley where he would sit and pray. He would read Scripture. Sometimes he would take others with him to this serene and tranquil place and they would spend extended time in prayer and worship. I found myself wishing I had such a place to retreat and be with Jesus.

About three years later, I was talking with a church leader who had been mentored by Juan Carlos. I mentioned how I had been inspired to find a special place to get away and meet with God each day.

To my surprise, the pastor laughed and quickly asked, "Did Juan Carlos tell you about the beautiful stream in the valley?" I affirmed that he had described a little brook that had become his quiet and sacred space. Again the pastor laughed. I asked him to let me in on what was so funny.

"I prayed with Juan Carlos in that place on many occasions, sometimes for hours!" He went on, "It was a rain-control ravine with a dribble of water running down to a drain below." As he described the place, from his perspective, a light went on in my mind and heart. To Juan Carlos, this place was beautiful, sacred, and peaceful. It was where he met with God face-to-face and knelt on holy ground. It was a brook, a stream, a fountain of God's presence.

To everyone else it was just a little canal to control the flow of rain and the drainage from nearby streets.

Where is your holy space? Is there a place you meet with God? It could be a chair in your living room, a place in your neighborhood, a local park, or even a water runoff area that becomes a stream of God's presence.

Susanna Wesley, mother of the great church leaders John and Charles Wesley, was the youngest of twenty-five children, and she raised a large family of her own. The story is told of times in the day when Susanna would feel the call to pray. She would sit in a chair in the kitchen and flip her apron up over her head to make a prayer tent. The children knew not to interrupt unless it was urgent. Her sacred place was under an apron!

The powerful rise early and go to bed late. They serve God, others, and their community tirelessly. Their heart is often in the right place, but they never shut off.

Powerless people are directed and controlled by the needs of the crowd. They can't say no. When someone demands that they show up and do something, they get to work, never thinking that the presence of a need does not always demand that they be the one to meet it.

Those who are *empowered* by God know how to work, serve, and care for others. They take delight in helping people in need and feel God's presence and strength as they extend the love of Jesus. But they also know how to walk away, find a quiet place, and rest. By a "quiet brook," under an apron, or just about anywhere will suffice. They are not forced into an endless cycle of labor by their own pride or the pressure of others. Instead, they live with a Christlike balance of service and rest. Because of this, they stay fresh, energized, and can be used for God's glory for a lifetime!

From the Heart of Jesus

Faithful and Fatigued Servant,

It is good to serve, give, and pour yourself out for others. This reveals the heart of God. Continue your faithful ministry of compassion and use your gifts to be a blessing to others.

But balance this with secret times away. Slow down, leave the crowds, disconnect, and seek the face of the One who made you. Open the Scriptures, talk with the Father, and find rest and refreshment in the arms of God.

You don't have the strength to serve endlessly and give without also receiving. And you don't have to meet every need that crosses your path.

If you really want to make an impact on the world around you, learn to balance passionate service and restful retreat.

▶▶ **Walk with Jesus** and learn more about how you can experience the balance of service and rest by reading Mark 1 and 6 and Luke 4:1–6:26.

Resources for Living an Empowered Life

Receiving the Strength You Need Today

We all need rest for our body, heart, mind, and soul. God has designed this rhythm of rest into the universe. Unfortunately, we often avoid the very things that can feed and fuel our lives. We push and push, thinking this honors God, but forget to balance hard work with rest, refreshment, and play.

When we walk closely with God, his presence fills our soul and empowers us for faithful living. As we watch the lives of great people of faith, we discover the value of Sabbath and rest. As we look at the life of Jesus, we see a discipline of making space and time to retire from the frenzy of busy days and find space to be away with the Father. As we live an empowered life, we will discover the value and gift of making space for Sabbath and rest in the rhythm of our life.

Here are some ideas, prayers, and activities that can help you experience God's power through developing a pattern of rest in the flow of your days and weeks.

Daily Reading Guide for Week 3 of *Empowered*

Use these daily Bible readings and chapters from *Empowered* to gain a solid biblical picture of people who have experienced drawing near to God and being strengthened through Sabbath and rest. Learn and be inspired as you enter into their story.

Day and Character	Bible Reading	Reading in *Empowered*
Day 1—God's Example	Genesis 1–2	Chapter 13
Day 2—Moses's Teaching	Exodus 20	Chapter 14
Day 3—Israel's Struggle	Exodus 16	Chapter 15
Day 4—David's Shepherd Psalm	Psalm 23 and John 10	Chapter 16
Day 5—Elijah's Turning Point	1 Kings 18:16–19:18	Chapter 17
Weekend—Jesus's Early Mornings	Mark 1	Chapter 18

Prayer Guide

Take time to pray using the following prompts and ask God to empower you in fresh new ways:

- Thank God for giving his children an example of rest and Sabbath.
- Praise God for his infinite power and how he shares it with ordinary people.
- Acknowledge to God that you know he calls his children to a rhythm of rest and confess where you have been rebellious and have run from his gift of Sabbath.
- Praise God for the many ways he has provided what you need and showed you his love in tangible ways.
- Reflect on the ways God has been your Good Shepherd and pray for a heart that longs to follow his leading as a loved sheep.

- Admit to God where you are feeling weary and worn out. Ask him to refresh your soul with what you need in this season of life.

- Thank Jesus for giving you an example of a life filled with passionate service, but also punctuated with quiet times away with the Father. Pray that you will be more like Jesus as you make space to retreat into quiet times in the presence of God.

Journal and Personal Reflections

Write some of your own thoughts and reflections on the following topics and questions:

If you could take a full day for Sabbath rest each week, what are some of the things you would do? How might these connect you with God?

_____

_____

_____

_____

_____

What gets in the way of your living a rested and refreshed life punctuated by quiet times with God?

_____

_____

_____

_____

_____

156

How can you make more space, daily and weekly, to pull away and seek the refreshment you need from God?

_____

_____

_____

_____

_____

Do you really believe God can provide all you need in six days of labor? Do you trust God to provide all you and your loved ones need? What drives you to keep working even on a day set aside for rest?

_____

_____

_____

_____

_____

Make a list of ways you have seen God be your Good Shepherd.

_____

_____

_____

_____

Make a list of ways you could and should follow him more closely as his loved sheep.

_____

_____

_____

_____

_____

Action Ideas

Use one or more of the following ideas or exercises to plug into God's power in the coming days:

A One-Month Experiment of Sabbath

Look at your schedule for the coming four weeks. Identify the best day for you to take a Sabbath. Sometimes this will overlap between two days (as it did in the ancient world where Sabbath was sundown Friday to sundown Saturday). You might not be able to block out a full twenty-four hours. Also, each person's Sabbath will look different. If you have young children, the idea of being alone for a full day may not be a legitimate option. But work at making a space to slow down, reflect, rest, and meet with God. When our three boys were young, my wife, Sherry, and I made the same day our Sabbath. She had a third of the day all to herself, I had a third of the day to myself, and we spent the other third of the day together with the boys. We tried to stay away from work in the office and at home and make this a day of refreshment.

Mini-Retreats

A mini-retreat might be pushing back from your desk or work for three minutes to say a prayer, connect with God, read a verse or two from the Bible, and ask God to empower you for the rest of the day.

It can be a five-to-ten-minute walk around the block to clear your mind and talk with Jesus.

It could be fifteen minutes in the cab of your truck during your lunch break listening to good Christian music and worshiping.

Come up with three ideas for a personal mini-retreat that you could slip into the flow of your day.

- _____

- _____

- _____

In the next week, try to go on one or two mini-retreats a day. Let these moments connect you with God and empower you to live more fully and passionately for him.

Grow as a Sheep

Take time to memorize Psalm 23 and use it as a prayer guide to ask God to help you see him more fully as your Good Shepherd and you as his loved sheep. Pray that you will follow more closely.

Take a Nap and Have a Snack

Find a time in the coming weeks when you could take a nap, have a snack, and ask God to draw near and refresh your soul. Let this be a spiritual discipline and more than just a time of physical rest. Before you take your nap, read Psalm 127 and ask God to help you know that he will take care of everything while you are resting.

SECTION 4

Propelled Onward by the Call and Mission of God

He said to them: "It is not for you to know the times or dates the Father has set by his own authority. But you will receive power when the Holy Spirit comes on you; and you will be my witnesses in Jerusalem, and in all Judea and Samaria, and to the ends of the earth."

Acts 1:7–8

Then Esther sent this reply to Mordecai: "Go, gather together all the Jews who are in Susa, and fast for me. Do not eat or drink for three days, night or day. I and my attendants will fast as you do. When this is done, I will go to the king, even though it is against the law. And if I perish, I perish."

Esther 4:15–16

19

Paul's Call

Knocked Down, Blinded, and Turned Around

"Then I asked, 'Who are you, Lord?'

"'I am Jesus, whom you are persecuting,' the Lord replied. 'Now get up and stand on your feet. I have appeared to you to appoint you as a servant and as a witness of what you have seen and will see of me. I will rescue you from your own people and from the Gentiles. I am sending you to them to open their eyes and turn them from darkness to light, and from the power of Satan to God, so that they may receive forgiveness of sins and a place among those who are sanctified by faith in me.'"

Acts 26:15–18

What were you doing when God revealed his presence and love to you? Where were you headed when God invited you to become a follower of Jesus? Do you remember? Were you five, fifteen, eighty-five?

I remember what I was doing. I was almost sixteen years old and my days were filled with adolescent meaning and significance. I was in pursuit of cute girls, good waves, any thrill I could experience

163

with friends, and whatever seemed like fun. Most of what caught my interest was illegal, immoral, ill-advised, or all three.

The summer I placed my trust in Jesus, everything changed. It was not like I eased off the gas pedal and turned the steering wheel of my life gently in a new direction. It was more like throwing the car into reverse while going full speed ahead. Virtually everything in my attitude, motives, and daily life started to change. It was not time for a minor adjustment or slight tweaks in my life goals. Everything needed an overhaul. It was time for a U-turn!

I think that is why I love the story of the apostle Paul's encounter with Jesus. His life was heading the wrong direction in even more blatant and heinous ways than mine was. Paul needed a completely new road map. He was on a mission, but it was diametrically opposed to the will and way of God.

What were you doing when God called you to lay down your sins and take up the amazing grace of Jesus Christ? What wrong road were you heading down?

The man we call the apostle Paul actually had a different name before he became a follower of Jesus. His name was Saul and he was invested forcefully in a number of things that dishonored God. He was destroying Christian families. He led a movement that was having church leaders killed. With vengeance Saul was seeking to obliterate the very name of Jesus from the face of the earth. His mission was clear: stomp out the growing Christian movement he hated. Saul saw Jesus as a threat and rival to his Jewish faith. He had a sense of call and mission but it was all in opposition to the message and ministry of Jesus.

We first meet Saul at an ancient public execution. Saul stood watch over the cloaks of the Jewish leaders as they beat a man named Stephen to death with stones.[1] Stephen was a Spirit-filled, wise, and godly leader in the early church.[2] He loved Jesus. He preached truth with power. His uncompromising integrity and bold proclamation of Jesus was seen as a threat by the religious establishment and they condemned him to death. They were so filled with fury that they personally acted as his executioners.

There was hatred in Saul's eyes and a deep feeling of self-righteous delight as he watched Stephen's lifeblood darken the ground. Can you see Stephen, the Spirit-filled preacher, sprawled at the feet of Saul, broken . . . bloody . . . his very life crushed out of him. There stood Saul, proudly giving the final stamp of approval at his execution.[3]

Sometime later Saul was marching toward Jerusalem with letters from the Jewish Supreme Court to dismantle churches and Christian families. He had an entourage of security and authorities to make sure he could fulfill his goal of crushing the people of the Way: followers of Jesus.[4]

While on his journey, Saul was suddenly knocked off his mount and blinded, and he heard a voice. Right there in the middle of the road, he met the living and resurrected Jesus Christ. He was given a new mission, a new calling, a new passion, and with time, a new name.

"Saul, you will preach the good news of this Jesus you were persecuting just moments ago! You will defend the Christian faith with your very life, convert everyone who will listen to your message, and gladly take abuse and suffer for the name of Jesus.

"Your family will be the people you persecuted. Some of them will fear you because you killed their loved ones and locked their family members in prison. You will kneel in prayer and sing songs of praise with people you hated and wanted dead."

After meeting Jesus on the road to Damascus, Saul was a new man. He was radically changed. From that time on, whenever Paul told his story of coming to faith in the Messiah, he would reflect on the condition of his life before his transformation and conversion. He declared, "I persecuted the followers of this Way to their death, arresting both men and women and throwing them in prison."[5] Paul also referred to himself as the "worst of sinners,"[6] because he knew his own personal history. He had a sense that if God could save, call, and use someone like him to proclaim the grace of Jesus, then God could use anyone.[7]

When Saul the Christian-killer became Paul the Christian leader, preacher, and church-planter, a new mission drove him forward with an unstoppable force. God called him and set his life on a new course . . . one he would never have dreamed possible.

God was calling this man to a whole new life: "Paul, you will give witness, for the rest of your days, to the very Jesus you denied and said was a fraud! You will preach the message of Jesus to both Jewish people (your own clan) and to the Gentiles (outsiders). God will use you to open eyes that are spiritually blind so that they might see the light and life of the Savior. As you go on your mission and follow Jesus, people will be set free from the power of Satan and come under the amazing strength of the Living God. As you tell your story and declare the true message of faith, people will be saved as they trust in Jesus and enter a lifelong process of spiritual growth and maturity."

It was this call, this mission, that drove Paul to the ends of the earth. It was this consuming passion that caused him to keep telling others about the Savior even when he was rejected, beaten with rods, stoned within an inch of his life, and strapped up five times to receive the forty lashes less one.

The beauty of Paul's story is that he laid down his life, dreams, and personal mission and took up the call of God. He followed Jesus no matter what the cost. He discovered that God's love was big enough to cover his sins. He learned that God had a mission and calling even for a man who had violently opposed the gospel of Jesus.

When I met Patrick, he was a gentle man with a quick wit, high energy, and a big laugh. He was part of the church I served, and when his name came up to be on our deacon board, everyone was very positive. He and his wife were serving in the children's ministry, they were generous with anyone in a time of need, and Patrick clearly loved Jesus.

It was not until he came on the deacon board and I spent time with him one-on-one that I learned who this man really was. Over a six-month period, I found out more and more about his past. He had grown up in a tough neighborhood in Boston and been a street brawler from his youth. He volunteered to fight in the Vietnam War, and his taste for battle and blood was so voracious that he was eventually discharged because killing came too easily for him.

When he returned to the States, he became a bodyguard for a cocaine dealer. This "occupational" move allowed him to have unfettered access to the three things he loved most at that point in his life: drugs, women, and violence. As Patrick would tell me on numerous occasions as we talked about his personal history, "I thought my life was great. I had everything! But then, I met Jesus."

This man had his life turned upside down. God broke through. I know this is not the normal way things go, but his love for drugs, his profane mind-set, and his love for violence melted way. His heart was transformed. He met a godly woman, got married, joined a church, worked hard at a non-drug-related job, and began a new life.

Patrick felt a call to ministry. Not full-time vocational church service, but a clear sense that he should serve others, help in the church, give things away, and tell others about Jesus's love and power. With that call firmly established in his heart, Patrick went to work each day as a missionary for Jesus. He invested his evenings and weekends in serving people in need. Like the apostle Paul, Patrick became a new person.

I can still remember the first time my wife, Sherry, and I went out on a date after our first son was born. We prayed about who we could entrust with our only child for a couple of quick hours as we tried to have a little time with just the two of us. We made a thoughtful decision, and that night we placed our son in the arms of a man who had been a violent killing machine, a bodyguard for a cocaine dealer, and a profane, womanizing drug addict.

As we pulled out of the driveway of Patrick and his wife's home, we both felt total peace. We knew our little boy Zach would be safe and well cared for. He was under the care of a gentle, good-hearted, generous, and tender man who had been transformed by Jesus. Patrick's old life was gone. He had heard the call of God, seen the face of Jesus, been filled with the Holy Spirit, and was empowered to serve in the name of the Savior. This was one of hundreds of times over the coming years that God would minister to me, my wife, and our family through this transformed man, his wife, and their family.

What were you doing when God reached down from the glory of heaven and touched your heart? What was the trajectory and direction of your life? How much has it changed? Has God set you on a new path? Has he given you a mission?

Of course he has!

When anyone says yes to Jesus, they begin a journey of following his mission and ways. The will of God becomes our way of life. The dreams of God invade our sleeping and our waking hours. The GPS of our soul is reprogrammed and our job is to listen and follow the next God-given direction.

The powerful set their life direction, hoist their sails, and off they go. No one or nothing is going to get them off their self-assigned course. They have plans, objectives, to-do lists, and a strategy of their own. Sometimes their mission is far from God's will.

The powerless go where the winds blow and don't have big goals or a life-mission statement. They simply follow the path of least resistance.

The *empowered* yield to the winds of the Holy Spirit. They hear the call of Jesus and follow. They don't have everything figured out, but they do know the One who sits on the throne of history and rules the universe. They know their past and recognize their sin. They admit their need of a Savior and gladly embrace the amazing grace of God offered through the death and resurrection of Jesus. Their past is behind them, forgiven, and cleansed. Their future is driven by a clear sense of call to share the same love, grace, and message of Jesus that has transformed their life.

From the Heart of Saul Who Became Paul

Fellow Rock Thrower,

We have all cast stones, hurt people, rebelled against God, and run from Jesus. We are all great sinners apart from the grace of Jesus. We all look in the rearview mirror of our life and feel deep shame for things we have thought, said, and done.

Forget what lies behind. Fix your eyes on the truth: In Jesus, you are now his saint. Through Jesus you are cleansed. Because of Jesus's death and glorious resurrection, you have a new life and mission.

Press forward, confident that the Holy Spirit dwells in you, God loves you, and Jesus calls you to be his messenger in this world. Don't say, "God could never speak through me or use me for his glory." Remember that a hate-filled, Christian-killing, Jesus-mocking man was called to start churches, preach the gospel, and write books of the Bible.

God can use you more than you can imagine. Just walk with Jesus, be available, and see what he does in and through you, for his glory.

▸▸ Walk with Saul/Paul and learn more about how you can be filled with the power of God through a clear sense of mission by reading Acts 7:1–8:3 and Acts 9, 22, 26.

20

Isaiah's Invitation

Speaking with Blistered Lips

In the year that King Uzziah died, I saw the Lord, high and exalted, seated on a throne; and the train of his robe filled the temple. Above him were seraphim, each with six wings: With two wings they covered their faces, with two they covered their feet, and with two they were flying. And they were calling to one another:

"Holy, holy, holy is the LORD Almighty;
the whole earth is full of his glory." . . .

Then one of the seraphim flew to me with a live coal in his hand, which he had taken with tongs from the altar. With it he touched my mouth and said, "See, this has touched your lips; your guilt is taken away and your sin atoned for."

Isaiah 6:1–3, 6–7

The king is dead.
Long live the King!
This is a simple summary of the opening verses of Isaiah chapter six.

The opening words are, "In the year that King Uzziah died." Uzziah was the leader of the southern kingdom of Judah and had sat on the throne in Jerusalem for fifty-two years. This is the equivalent of thirteen presidential terms of office.

I am fifty-two years old at the publication of this book. When I was born, JFK was president and nine presidents have served since then. Imagine a nation with the same political leader in office for fifty-two years.

To top it off, Uzziah (sometimes called Azariah) had been a great king. Every monarch of both the northern kingdom of Israel and the southern kingdom of Judah was given a summary declaration at the end of their life. We are told they either did "what was right in the eyes of the LORD," or "what was evil in the eyes of the LORD." Uzziah was one of the good guys![1]

Now the king was dead. Uzziah was no longer on the throne.

More than five decades of virtuous leadership was now in their national rearview mirror and the people of Judah were fearful about their future. Most of them could not remember anyone leading the nation except Uzziah. Who would watch over them, protect their nation, and point the way forward? The king was dead. The throne was empty. Their future was uncertain.

The king is dead.

Long live the King!

In the same breath Isaiah brought hope to the people of God. King Uzziah was dead, but the King of glory, the Lord of eternity, was still on his heavenly throne. Long live the King of heaven! Isaiah had a vision of the One who is high, exalted, and sovereign over the universe.

What a contrast!

Uzziah's reign was fifty-two years, Yahweh's rule is eternal. Uzziah was dead and buried. God is high and lifted up. Earthly kings come and go, the Maker of heaven and earth is sovereign over all time. The candle of King Uzziah was snuffed out, but the glorious light of God was still burning bright.

As the veil of heaven was pulled back, the prophet Isaiah saw a vision of angelic beings flying around the throne of God, and he heard them calling, "Holy, holy, holy is the LORD Almighty; the whole earth is full of his glory."[2] Smoke filled the temple. As the angelic declaration was lifted up, it seemed as if the very thresholds of heaven were about to come tumbling down. Everything was shaking, like a heavenly earthquake.

So much for fluffy clouds and quiet harp-playing angels! This heavenly vision revealed the glory of God and a passionate song being lifted to him in a magnificent refrain of eternal worship.

As Isaiah looked and listened, something happened inside the prophet. He saw himself in the light of the piercing, three-times holiness of God. The prophet became instantaneously aware of the condition of his heart and the depth of his need for cleansing.

Isaiah was ruined.

He was undone.

All thoughts of self-sufficiency came crumbling to the ground in the heaven-quake of God's glory. All reliance on personal power, thoughts of worthiness, or hopes of accomplishing something to make himself clean in the sight of this holy God went up in smoke. A spiritual mirror was placed before Isaiah, his eyes were opened, and he saw himself in the light of the glory of the King of all kings.

"Woe to me!" the prophet cried.[3] Translate: In myself, all is hopeless!

"I am ruined!" Translate: God's holiness is consuming me.

"I am a man of unclean lips." We can understand this: I am dirty, profane, profoundly sinful, and could never cleanse myself.

"I live among a people of unclean lips." There is no one good enough to stand before this God. Every person I have ever met is wholly unholy and utterly unworthy.

"My eyes have seen the King, the LORD Almighty." I have been given a momentary glimpse of God's glory and I will never be the same.

Have you ever stood in this place? Amazed and overwhelmed by the spectacular splendor of the living God? You might not have seen the angelic beings or felt heaven shuddering under the infinite weight of God's glory, but you were given a peek behind the veil. Have you stood, kneeled, or fallen flat on your face in awe of the one true God who is "holy, holy, holy"? Have you encountered the Lord of heaven with such intimacy and intensity that he gave you the gift of seeing your true self in the mirror of the burning radiance of his glory?

If you have, you understand Isaiah's response. Maybe you have said the same sort of thing to God, in your own words.

"I could die."

"I am coming apart!"

"I am impure, unclean, and sinful."

"This world is broken, filthy, and corrupt."

"I see you, God, with my blurred and tear-filled eyes, and I don't know what to do."

In these moments only God can save. On the brink of spiritual collapse and painful awareness of our profanity and our world's depravity, the only path to salvation is the grace of God.

As Isaiah trembled and quaked before the burning holiness of God, as he cringed at the painful reality of the degenerate condition of his soul, God intervened. The Lord of glory sent a messenger, an angelic being carrying grace disguised as a burning coal. Before Isaiah knew what was happening, the glowing orange ember was pressed against his lips and the smell of seared flesh filled the air. A cathartic touch of God was followed by these words:

See, this has touched your lips; your guilt is taken away and your sin atoned for.[4]

Have you felt the searing heat of God's grace? Have you smelled the burning flesh of your own lips being scorched by the holiness of God? If you have stood at the foot of the cross and looked into the holy, holy, holy face of the only Son of God, you have a sense of what Isaiah experienced. Only when we kneel before Emmanuel, God with us, and see his redemptive suffering, can we also feel the red-hot forgiveness revealed on the cross. When we cry, "I am unclean, I am a descendant of a sinful race of people, I am undone, I can't fix myself," we finally see ourselves as we are.

This is when Jesus reaches out to us with his nail-pierced hands and touches us. His redemptive blood, shed on the cross for us, is placed on us as the final Passover sacrifice. Our guilt is taken away. Our sin is atoned for.

When Isaiah heard these words, he also felt the weight of sin being lifted by the cosmic hands of God. Now he was ready to receive a call. It was time to discover his mission. The prophet heard the voice of God ask two life-changing questions: "Whom shall I send?" and "Who will go for us?"[5]

I don't know how he would have responded before his life-changing encounter with the Divine One. But now, through mangled, seared, and swollen lips, Isaiah muttered, "Here am I. Send me!"[6]

In the glow of the heavenly King's holiness, profoundly aware of his own sinfulness, with blistered lips being healed by the touch of God, Isaiah was ready to follow God in a new way. Now he could speak *for* the Divine One. He was ready to bear the burden of God's call for him to proclaim heavenly truth to a rebellious and resistant people.

Is our call to follow and live for Jesus any different? When we have seen the face of the glorious Lord of the universe, quaked in the presence of his power, become painfully aware of the filth in our own soul, and been cleansed by the burning grace of Jesus Christ, we are ready to hear the invitation. We are empowered and propelled forward by the very presence of God.

"Whom shall I send? And who will go for us?"

"Therefore go and make disciples of all nations, baptizing them in the name of the Father and of the Son and of the Holy Spirit, and teaching them to obey everything I have commanded you."[7]

"But you will receive power when the Holy Spirit comes on you; and you will be my witnesses."[8]

A call, a life mission, a reason to live in this broken and fractured world is found only when we encounter God as he is, so we can see ourselves as we are. When this happens, we are changed and become vessels God can pour his grace in and through. The truth is, God has no perfect vessels to use in this world. He has broken jars of clay that have been put back together by his amazing grace. As the holy God of heaven fills us, his love pours out of the cracks in our lives and refreshes others.

The powerful get glimpses of God's glory and recoil. They do not want to see themselves in the light of heavenly holiness. They stand resistant and refuse to fall on their face in the presence of the Almighty. The idea of a broken heart and blistered lips does not fit their idea of being in control of their faith.

The powerless can see their own depravity but can't imagine a God who would still love them, save them, and use them for his purposes in this world. They stay on the sidelines of life and refuse to serve because they feel unworthy and inadequate.

The *empowered* are profoundly aware of God's holiness, their own sinfulness, and the hope of healing that is found in Jesus, the Christ. They know that they are not worthy. They are broken and humble. They are also empowered and passionate. Their lips have felt the searing burn of coals from a heavenly altar. The blood of the Lamb, who takes away the sins of the world, has cleansed their soul.

Each day they feel the empowering presence of the God who is holy, holy, holy and they say again, "Here I am, send me."

From the Heart of Isaiah

Worshiper of the King,

Keep your eyes on heaven and see the King of glory lifted up. Don't let your heart and eyes fixate on thrones, oval offices, or seats of power on this earth. Human leaders come and go, but the King of all kings rules and reigns eternally.

Come near to the true Ruler of the universe. Though your knees buckle under the sheer glory of his holiness, though all heaven quakes under the force of his presence, draw near. Confess your sins, let the coal touch your lips, be cleansed by the grace of God. Look into the face of the crucified and risen Lord and know that his grace is yours by faith.

You will be undone. In his presence you will be changed, broken, emptied, and filled. You will see Jesus and you will never be the same.

Then, when the God of heaven calls you to go, serve, love, to give, sacrifice, and follow, you will boldly declare, "Here I am, Lord, send me!"

▸▸ **Walk with Isaiah** and learn more about receiving heavenly cleansing and power in the presence of God by reading Isaiah 6.

21

Abraham's Journey

Going without Knowing

The LORD had said to Abram, "Go from your country, your people and your father's household to the land I will show you."

Genesis 12:1

"Go to the land I will show you."

That was the call of an unknown God to a seventy-five-year-old man and his family. "Pack up all you have and start walking. Travel until I tell you to stop. I have a land for you and your descendants, but I will not tell you exactly where it is until you get there."

Can you fathom this kind of spiritual conversation? It reads like a comedy routine more than a sacred text.

God: Abram, it's me, God.

Abram: God who?

God: Your God.

Abram: (Cautiously) Nice to meet you.

God: I have one quick directive for you.

177

Abram: (More cautiously) What do you have in mind?

God: Pack up your wife, family, and everything you own and start traveling. I have a great land for you. Just keep hiking until I tell you to stop. It's going to be great! Trust me.

Abram: What's wrong with Ur? This is where all my family has lived for generations.

God: I have a special land for you. I have a plan to do great things in and through you. Your part is to trust me, pack up, and start walking. I will be with you and will bless you.

Abram: (After a time of silence and reflection) OK, I'm in. I'll let my wife know.

In any generation this story is shocking. Who would pack up everything to follow an unknown God to an unknown location with an uncertain future?

Abram did!

He did not just move a few miles across town. It was not a ten-mile journey that would allow him and his family to go back and see family for a long weekend. The distance from Ur (Abram's homeland) to Canaan (the Promised Land) was over five hundred miles as a bird flies. The most common travel route was along the Euphrates River. The trip went through rugged and desolate land, and with all the twists and turns on the path, it was closer to a thousand-mile trip. Imagine walking from Washington DC to Miami, Florida, and you might get the idea.

Who does this? Who trusts God and begins traveling before they know the destination? Can you imagine Abram and his family a hundred miles into the trip and wondering, "Are we there yet? How long will this trip take?" Can you hear Sarai, Abram's wife, asking, "Do you have some kind of directions? Is there a final destination? How will we know when we have arrived?"

Just like modern husbands and wives might argue on a road trip in a minivan, we have to believe that Abram and Sarai had a few heated discussions along the way. They were not in a vehicle with air-conditioning, on smoothly paved roads, with movies to entertain the kids. They were in a caravan traveling over rugged roads, in a desert, carrying all they owned, and no one was exactly sure where they were going.

Who follows God like this? Who hears a call, leaves everything, and begins walking? What kind of madness is this? At the 500-mile mark, the 700-mile mark, and as they approached 1,000 miles of travel, was there a point where Abram, Sarai, and their family said, "Maybe we should do a quick U-turn and head back to Ur"?

The truth is, Abram had encountered the presence of God and was driven by a call and a promise.[1] God told Abram that he would be blessed and become a great nation of people. His name would be great. And he would become a blessing to all the people of the earth. With a call to follow and a promise of blessing, Abram kept walking.

After more than a thousand miles of rugged topography, the weary travelers arrived in Canaan. When they finally reached their destination, God appeared to Abram again and told him, "To your offspring I will give *this* land."[2] They were home! But home was a land they had never seen before.

Abram was three quarters of a century old when this all happened. Twenty-somethings and newlyweds are often game to live on the edge and take risks. People racing toward becoming an octogenarian are not usually as ripe for adventure. But something in Abram drove him forward, toward a new land and a God he would come to know very, very well—One who would give him a new name, Abraham, the father of many nations.. The first thing he did when they arrived in this new land was build an altar to the Lord and worship this God he had followed by faith almost a thousand miles.[3]

Times have changed. We like plans and certainty. We travel with a GPS, know the final destination, and even get moment-by-moment updates on exactly when we will arrive. In our technology-laden culture we don't have to worry much about getting lost along the way. If we get even slightly off the prescribed route, there is a recalculation and a gentle voice on a GPS that gives an updated route provided in real time.

Who, in today's world, would actually go without knowing? Who would pack up their life and start hiking? Is there anyone left who will seek to follow God with a faith that takes risks and counts the cost?

The answer to these questions might shock you. Who would follow like this? You and me! Every person who says yes to Jesus and becomes his disciple does exactly what Abraham did. We pack up all we have, all we are, and every dream we hold in our heart, and we start walking.

We follow Jesus.

We don't know where God will take us. We really have no idea what route we will travel. We are not informed as to our final destination (on this earth). This is what it means to be a Christian. Not one of us says yes to Jesus and then hands him our map, plans, and objectives and tells the Savior what route we prefer. We follow in his footsteps.[4]

As it was in Abraham's day, so it was in Jesus's day. When the Lord called people to become his disciples, he simply said, "Come, follow me."[5] Simon Peter and his brother Andrew had no idea what this would mean and where it would lead them, but "immediately they left the boat and their father and followed him."[6]

History tells us that both Andrew and Peter were crucified because they followed the Savior. Had they been aware of this at the start of the journey, they might have thought twice before dropping their nets and leaving the family fishing business. But followers of Jesus don't know the exact route, we just fix our eyes on the Savior and keep on walking.

As it was in Abraham's day, and in the days of Jesus, so it is today. There is no way to follow Jesus other than counting the cost, taking a risk, and walking with the Lord. We follow him, no matter where he leads and no matter what we are called to do. We don't have an end game. We are not given a spiritual GPS that assures us we will arrive at our destination unscathed and on time. Instead, Jesus says, "Whoever wants to be my disciple must deny themselves and take up their cross daily and follow me. For whoever wants to save their life will lose it, but whoever loses their life for me will save it."[7]

That is the call, the invitation, the way of faith.

Who follows God like this? Abraham and Sarah. Peter and Andrew. You and me. We hear his call. He leads us on a mission day-by-day and moment-by-moment. We go, not knowing where it will lead us, but trusting the God who calls us to follow him.

The powerful make plans and follow them rigorously. They plug in the desired destination into the GPS of their life and execute their plan flawlessly. They might even ask for God's blessing and invite Jesus to tag along on their journey.

The powerless feel that all of life is a mystery. They are a ship cut loose from all moorings and fate blows them wherever it will. They don't live with a confidence that God is in charge of the universe or their life. They are uncertain and fearful.

Empowered people don't make their plans and then ask God to bless them. Instead they walk in step with the Holy Spirit. They live by faith and know that God can see the end of the road even when they can't. They live with tenacious trust and fearless faith that allows them to take one step at a time. Like Abraham, they pack up, start walking, and travel with God, trusting that he will lead them to exactly where he wants them to go. Like Peter and Andrew, they drop their nets and follow the Savior. Like countless Christians through the centuries, they follow God on a journey of faith that often means going forward without knowing exactly where God is taking them.

From the Heart of Abraham

Fellow Traveler,

God's ways are not our ways. His call is rarely conventional and it does not always make sense when we first hear it. The road he calls us to walk can be long, it can seem like a detour, and sometimes we wonder if we are even on the right path!

In those moments, remember his call, hold on to his promises, and watch for his blessings. When the terrain is rugged and you feel weary, realize that you are not alone. His presence is with you. You might not know exactly where he is leading you, but you can know that God is with you, and that will be enough.

▸▸ **Walk with Abraham** and learn more about following God on the journey of faith by reading Genesis 11–12 and 17.

22

Esther's Risk

This Could Cost You Everything

Then Esther sent this reply to Mordecai: "Go, gather together all the Jews who are in Susa, and fast for me. Do not eat or drink for three days, night or day. I and my attendants will fast as you do. When this is done, I will go to the king, even though it is against the law. And if I perish, I perish."

Esther 4:15–16

Have you ever been called to do something risky, dangerous, and clearly beyond your own ability? Esther knew that feeling and had to make a decision that could cost her everything, including her own life.

To understand the danger of Esther's mission, we have to go back to the beginning of the book of the Bible that bears her name. We must understand the culture in which she lived. The book of Esther was written long before the advent of women's liberation. It would be thousands of years before the concept of equality for women showed up on the cultural landscape. Women had no rights and no authority in society at the time the book of Esther was

183

written. It was not a matter of discussing if women could vote. This was a nonissue. Women were not even allowed to speak in public settings. It was an utterly male-dominated society.

In the beginning of the book of Esther, we read a story about the king of Persia, Xerxes. He called for his wife, Vashti, to come join him at his great banquet. She did something unthinkable in her day and culture. She refused![1]

After a quick consultation with his political cabinet, the king made a decision to remove her from her royal position and Vashti lost her crown. She was never allowed to enter the presence of the king (her husband) again! This might seem barbaric and unthinkable to the modern mind, but this was the law of the land in the days of Esther.[2]

The king decided it was time to find a new queen, so he did a national search. He began a show called *The Bachelorette, Persia Edition*. The king's servants gathered the most beautiful women from every corner of the kingdom. Like all reality shows, there were many episodes and lots of women were lined up to do all they could to impress the king. When it was all said and done, one woman was crowned winner and became the new queen of the land. Her name was Esther and she was a good Jewish girl. As was the case in her day, Esther had no say in any of this.[3]

As we continue reading the book of Esther, we find the new queen in a dilemma. The king had signed an edict that every Jew in the country of Persia, on one day, would be slaughtered. He was not even aware that his new wife had Jewish blood in her veins and a family tree with deep roots in the religion of Yahweh. Nonetheless, the political edict he had signed placed a certain death sentence on all of the Jewish people living in the 127 provinces of the Persian Empire, including his own wife and queen.[4]

Esther's uncle Mordecai came to her with a challenge, a mission from God. He exhorted Esther to enter the presence of the great King Xerxes and plead for the lives of her people. Esther explained to Mordecai that she was not at liberty to come into the presence of the king without being summoned. As was the law, anyone who approached the king without an invitation was executed on the spot, unless Xerxes raised his scepter, allowing them in, and sparing their life. Esther reported to Mordecai that she had not been summoned into the presence of the king for a whole month.[5]

Mordecai's response was *not* gentle or kind. It was prophetic and clear.

> Do not think that because you are in the king's house you alone of all the Jews will escape. For if you remain silent at this time, relief and deliverance for the Jews will arise from another place, but you and your father's family will perish. And who knows but that you have come to your royal position for such a time as this? (Esther 4:13–14)

This was a desperate situation and Mordecai wondered if Esther had been placed right where she was for this very moment in history. Perhaps the God of the universe had arranged her location, relationship, and potential influence for the purpose of saving his people.

Perhaps.

Have you ever found yourself in a place or situation that seemed out of place? You wondered why you were there. You might have questioned if there was any reason you should stay where you were. Then, months or years later, it became clear that God had put you exactly where you were. The fog lifted and you could see that God had positioned you right where you were because he had a plan to use you and bring glory to himself. Have you ever had an epiphany and suddenly realized, *This is no accident, I am part of a bigger plan orchestrated by the very hand of God*?

Mordecai planted a seed, an idea in the heart and mind of Esther. He was confident that God would somehow deliver the people of Israel, but he wondered if Esther would want to be part of this great work. Mordecai invited Queen Esther to believe there was more going on than met the eye. God was up to something bigger than her winning a beauty contest.

Don't you love Mordecai's spirit and faith in Yahweh? "I know God will deliver us. No doubt!" The question was not "Is God faithful?" The real issue was "Do you want to be part of God's mighty and miraculous work? Will you quiet your heart, unplug your ears, and receive what God has to say? Will you dare to walk to the door of the king's chamber, knock, and see if he raises the scepter and lets you in?"

Esther's response was not some knee-jerk decision to run over to chat with Xerxes. She took this moment very seriously. She asked all the Jews in the capital city of Susa to fast. There was a sense that they needed to seek the face of God with her for wisdom, strength, and courage as she pressed forward with her mission. She asked them to fast for three days and nights. This was a serious commitment. Esther committed that, after three days of seeking the face of God, she would walk to the throne room of the king and stand in the entry. She knew that one of two things would happen: she would be invited in or executed.

Her final words ring through history, "And if I perish, I perish."

What commitment! What a resolute spirit! What a risk!

Are you facing a moment where you might be tempted to take the easy way out? If not, you will. Probably sooner than you think. That is the reality of being a follower of God. Our Savior faced intense suffering and persecution. So will we. If we walk closely with him, this will be part of the journey. For Esther, faithfulness to God could mean giving up her life.

When you face life's challenging moments, don't do it alone. Don't try to stand in your own strength. Invite others to gather around you, to fast, pray, and support you. God has placed us in community so we can help each other in these moments. Be willing to count the cost. Clarify the will of God and his mission for you and press forward, no matter what you face.

The powerful face life's challenging and critical moments and believe their superior mental acuity, personal resolve, and internal reserve of strength will help them make the right choices and stand strong through the hard times. They are committed to accomplish the mission no matter what. But they seek to do this alone.

The powerless hear the edict of the king, get the bad news, and crumble. They are sure they can't make it through and they don't really know if there is a God big enough to overcome the power of Xerxes. They feel alone and don't think to gather people around them to offer support, wisdom, and help.

The *empowered* hear the call of God and know they can't deliver the goods and make it happen. They also believe that, with the help of God's people, it can be done. They fast and pray, they look to God for strength, and they press on, knowing that God is big enough to accomplish his will in and through ordinary people. They are confident that if God could use a young Jewish woman in a foreign land, he can use someone like me.

Will you join the tribe of Esther and say, "I will follow God's call and mission"? Will you gather people around you to undergird you with strength and support in the hard times? Will you stand up boldly and pursue God's will and mission as you say, "If I perish, I perish!"

From the Heart of Esther

Desperate Friends,

We are not in control, not one of us. The powers of this world are mighty and they seek to manipulate our lives. Yet through it all, God is still on the throne. Powerful people make decisions and they seem to be in charge, but at the end of the day you will see that God is sovereign over kings, kingdoms, you, and me.

Perhaps God has placed you right where you are for his sake and for a greater plan. It might be that following him includes taking some risks . . . big risks. You might be looking for a quick and easy way out.

Seek the face of God, gather people to pray with you, and clarify God's will for your life. When you have confidence that you are pursuing God's mission, go for it. Count the cost and follow fearlessly and fiercely. Hold the hand of God and declare, "If I perish, I perish, but I will serve God and accomplish his mission, even if it costs me everything."

▸▸ **Walk with Esther** and learn more about following the call of God even when it is dangerous and uncertain as you read the book of Esther.

23

Mary's Maternity

I Am the Lord's Servant

I am the Lord's servant. . . .
May your word to me be fulfilled.

Luke 1:38

It was the best of times!

She was a young woman.

She was engaged to be married.

She had been faithful to God and had remained a virgin.

This young woman had her whole life laid out like a blank canvas ready for God to paint her future. What dreams ran through her mind? She must have wondered what it would be like to be married. The wedding would be a simple, but wonderful celebration. Of course they would have children. Maybe a son to work in Joseph's carpentry business. They would probably live in Nazareth, an obscure little town with one stoplight in the region of Galilee.

Mary's dreams for the future would have been simple, tame, and nothing terribly exotic. Not much really happened in Nazareth. Nobody significant or famous came from this sleepy backwater town . . . and the people of Nazareth liked it that way!

Enter the angel Gabriel.[1]

The glorious heavenly warrior showed up in Nazareth. He appeared to Mary and brought a divine message. "Greetings, you who are highly favored! The Lord is with you." Mary would have responded with great fear, as did virtually every mortal who encountered an angel. Every angel is taught the simple greeting, "Fear not," for a good reason. The normal response to encountering an angelic being was raw terror—some people even passed out!

We read that Mary was "greatly troubled." So the heavenly messenger followed up his initial greeting with the customary "Do not be afraid." It seemed to work, because Mary entered a conversation with Gabriel.

The heavenly messenger proceeded to relay a message to this young engaged woman that would have been exciting, unbelievable, and troubling all at the same time. Try to forget that you have heard the Christmas story year after year. Block out of your mind all of the iconic paintings of Mary holding the baby Jesus and seeming quite peaceful and content. Imagine a young country girl who is engaged, a virgin, and not used to angels showing up with messages from God.

These were the items Gabriel had on his checklist to communicate to Mary:

Mary, you have found favor with God. This would have delighted her since she was truly seeking to be faithful.

You will conceive and give birth to a son. This would have been good news in a year or two, but Mary was not married and Joseph might have some concerns about this. Not to mention she had never been intimate with a man.

You will call your son Jesus. Mary probably had some ideas of names for her first son, but the angel seemed very insistent about this point.

Your son will be great. What mother does not desire greatness for her children?

Your boy will be called the Son of the Most High. Now this is something. She was thinking Joseph would be the father of all her children. Now it seems her firstborn son would be fathered by God. How do you get your mind around this idea?

Your son Jesus will receive the throne of the ancient King David as a gift from God. Mary knew the stories of the great King David. He had ruled over the united nation of Israel back in the glory days. She knew that her people were longing and praying for a new king to arise from the line of David and free them from the oppression of the Romans. She also knew that her fiancée, Joseph, was a descendant of David.[2] This must have all been swirling around in her mind.

He will reign as the King over all of Jacob's descendants forever. Jacob was the third of the great patriarchs of the faith, following Abraham and Isaac. How would the son of a peasant girl from Nazareth qualify for such a high calling?

The kingdom her son Jesus would rule was going to be eternal. What does a young girl do with this information? Her unborn baby would become a king who rules everything in the universe forever. She was a virgin. Her life plans and objectives didn't go beyond the borders of Galilee. Now she is talking to an angel and being told that her son would be the Eternal King of a never-ending kingdom.

This message was beyond Mary's wildest imagination. She could not comprehend fully what the heavenly messenger was describing. But, she did not debate the theology of the Messiah's eternal rule or ask for details about how her son could possibly ascend to this lofty place. Her follow-up question was quite simple and pragmatic.

"I am a virgin, I have never been with a man. How will this be?" Fair question!

Gabriel clarified as best he could. And theologians have been writing about it ever since. Here is the description of what is called "The Virgin Birth of Jesus." It has never happened before and will never happen again in human history. The angel said, "The

Holy Spirit will come on you, and the power of the Most High will overshadow you. So the holy one to be born will be called the Son of God" (Luke 1:35). Legions of pastors and theologians have tried to parse, preach, explain, and sort out exactly how this worked. The truth is, no one but God really knows. Articles and countless books have been written on this topic and it is still a mystery locked away in heaven.

The young peasant virgin did not ask for any additional clarity. Her response was humbling and beautiful in its simplicity. "I am the Lord's servant. May your word to me be fulfilled."

This was Mary's missionary moment. It was her call.

Mary would conceive a child before she was married and not be able to adequately explain how this happened. The people in her hometown would not approve or understand. Let's be honest, who was going to believe her story that an angel spoke to her and that God impregnated her? Mary would have known that many of her friends and neighbors would look at her with judgmental glares and whisper about her pregnancy. But she was still bold to offer herself as a servant who was ready to say, "May your word to me be fulfilled."

She would need to explain to her fiancé, Joseph, that she really had been faithful to him. She would have to convince him about the angel and her chastity and that her child would be the one and only Son of God! She did not know if he would break off their engagement, accuse her of unfaithfulness, or believe the true story of God's miraculous work in her life. Facing possible rejection by the man she loved, Mary was still confident to place her future in the hands of God.

With personal questions, societal judgment, and relational uncertainty, Mary's response was staggering: *"I am the Lord's servant. May your word to me be fulfilled."*

For some people, talk of Mary is often neglected, avoided, or underplayed. For others, there is an overemphasis on the young virgin. But when we read her story closely and learn of her deep faith and exemplary courage, we should admire, celebrate, and learn from this young girl. Worship is reserved for God alone, but respect and honor for a great woman who trusted God beyond understanding is entirely appropriate.

It was the best of times!

She was a young woman.

She was engaged to be married.

She had been faithful to God and remained a virgin.

She was pregnant with the Son of God!

Never forget that when God called Mary and informed her that every plan she had for the future was about to change, her response was, *"I am the Lord's servant. May your word to me be fulfilled."*

The powerful have their dreams and plans and no one is going to push them off their self-prescribed track. Not circumstances, not other people, not angels, not even God! They think they know what the future should hold for them and they pursue their plans no matter what.

The powerless have stopped dreaming. Their dreams and God's dreams don't seem worth pursuing. They have faced times when their dreams have been shattered and their hopes tattered. Now they guard their heart by refusing to embrace any dreams at all.

The *empowered* have a sense of the future and they dream of what could be. At the same time, their ears are open to the voice of God and their lives are always ready for adjustments according to the call and mission God has for them. They are ready to say, with Mary, *"I am the Lord's servant. May your word to me be fulfilled."* Then, when God reveals his will and plan, they follow with confidence and hope.

From the Heart of Mary

To Ordinary People,

Sometimes God's will for your life and his mission sneak up on you unexpectedly. You are living your ordinary life, doing ordinary things, in an ordinary place. All of a sudden, God shows up. He calls. He speaks. He sets your life on a new course . . . one you would never have imagined.

In these moments you might feel fearful, troubled, and uncertain. Listen for the voice of the Lord. Hear him say, "Don't be afraid."

Then, follow. With all your might, follow him. Let Jesus be formed in you, through whatever you face: uncertainty, embarrassment, anxiety, excitement, joy, and expectation. Just follow the leading of God and invite his will to be done. Ask Jesus to grow in you with each passing day.

When you wonder, who am I? Why would God use me? How can an ordinary person be used greatly by God? Remember, God loves common folks. Just look up and say to God, "I am the Lord's servant, may your word to me be fulfilled."

▶▶ **Walk with Mary** and learn more about how God calls and uses ordinary people to do great things by reading Matthew 1–2 and Luke 1–2.

24

Jesus's Mission

Seeking and Saving the Lost

For the Son of Man came to seek and save the lost.

Luke 19:10

If Jesus had a website, I believe the banner across the top of the home page should have his life mission statement in bold letters:

For the Son of Man came to seek and save the lost

Before Jesus left the glory of heaven, emptied himself, and prepared to enter human history, this was his vision. When Jesus walked on the earth, this was his mission. As Jesus hung on the cross dying for our sins and being punished in our place, this was his consuming passion. Even now, after his resurrection and ascension, Jesus still intercedes for us.[1] Seeking and saving the lost is eternally Jesus's passion.

The most common name Jesus used to describe himself was "the Son of Man." In Luke 19 we read the story of Jesus watching a sinful and self-centered man being transformed by his grace and

195

ushered into God's eternal family. Salvation descended on Zacchaeus from heaven and he was a changed man. In response, like a victory cry, Jesus declared his eternal mission statement, "For the Son of Man came to seek and save the lost." You can almost see the triumphant smile of God beam across the face of Jesus as he made this announcement.

It was this mission that caused Jesus to leave glory and enter history as a human being.[2] He came to live a sinless and perfect life. Jesus experienced what every human being experiences, without any compromise of disobedience to the Father; he never sinned.

Can we be certain that Jesus knew what humiliation, pain, and rejection awaited him on this earth? Absolutely. He knew exactly why he came and what he would experience.

Jesus was the Lamb of God who was slain before the creation of the earth.[3] He came to die. He knew what he would face. His mission drove him forward, even when it made no sense from a human perspective.

Jesus knew the physical pain he would endure and suffer. The God who made the heavens and the earth would be pressed through the birth canal of a virgin girl and be placed in the calloused and rugged hands of a carpenter. Jesus would feel hunger, cold, the irritation of a sliver in his skin, the sting of a stubbed toe, and the piercing pain of a carpenter's hammer missing the nail and hitting his thumb. He was sinless, but still fully human. Do you think Jesus grew up in a carpenter's home and hit every single nail on the head? It is not sinful to miss a nail and hit your thumb. It is painfully human.

The real question is not, did Jesus suffer? We know he did. The question we must answer is, Why? Why would Jesus leave heaven, take on flesh, and allow sinful people to abuse and mutilate his body? Why would he endure while friends abandoned and strangers mocked? Why would Jesus allow himself to suffer spiritual abandonment? Why would he come to this earth knowing all of this was going to happen?

The answer comes in one word: mission.

Jesus had a mission. He knew we were lost. He knew us by name and loved us before time began. Jesus was eternally aware that the only way you and I could come home to the Father and find cleansing from our sins was for him to die in our place, for our sins, on the cross. Jesus came to seek and save the lost. He endured it all for you! You are the answer to the question, Why?

Jesus also knew emotional and relational pain. He was often misunderstood and rejected. Some of his own family members accused him of being mentally unstable.[4] They did not understand his mission, but wanted to protect him from himself. The religious leaders, who should have recognized him as the Messiah, accused Jesus of being demon possessed and they plotted his destruction.[5] On his journey to the cross, Jesus watched the crowds that had adored him reveal their fickle nature and turn against him. Their cries of "Hosanna, blessed is he who comes in the name of the Lord" had just echoed through the hills outside of Jerusalem.[6] Now the crowd was crying, "Crucify!"[7]

In his greatest hour of need, the closest friends of Jesus abandoned him, every one of them fled.[8] Peter would deny Jesus three times, clearly and emphatically.[9] Judas, one of the twelve, would sell him for thirty pieces of silver.[10] Even his closest friends melted when the heat was on. Jesus felt the same emotional pain you or I would have if our dearest friends abandoned us in our hour of need.

Why would Jesus keep pressing on? The lost people Jesus was seeking to save did not show appreciation for his sacrifice. They showed no devotion to him. Why didn't Jesus just call down the angels of heaven and wipe out those who were brutalizing him? When Jesus was in the garden, he assured his disciples that he could call on his Father and with one request have twelve legions of angels show up and defend him. He could have stopped his suffering at any time.[11]

Can you picture it, 72,000 angels descending from heaven armed for battle?[12] One angel could have crushed those who were attacking Jesus. Jesus himself was the Lord over all the angels of heaven. He could have spoken one word and all of the unworthy, brutal, and sinful people in Jerusalem would have been wiped off the face of the earth.

He did not. He would not.

Jesus refused to call the angelic armies to his side. He did not defend himself. Through the physical and emotional abuse, Jesus pressed on toward the cross. The mission was too important. He had come to seek and save the lost and he was driven by this vision. Nothing would stop him.

What we often miss when we look at the suffering and passion of Jesus is that the physical, emotional, and relational pain Jesus endured were small in comparison to the spiritual suffering.

The spiritual suffering Jesus embraced on the cross was infinite in nature. All the sins of all people in history who would receive Jesus were placed on the suffering Savior as if they were his own. We can't begin to imagine the weight, guilt, and raw profanity of what Jesus endured. The sinless, spotless, perfectly holy Lamb of God, at one moment, had all of our sins poured on him.

It did not end there. As our sins became his, the infinite wrath and punishment we deserved fell on Jesus. He not only took the weight of our sins but the depth of our judgment. The holy and just wrath of heaven fell on Jesus and not on us.[13]

At that moment in time, the fellowship of the Trinity, in a way we can't fully comprehend, was ruptured. Jesus, who had been in eternal, ceaseless, and glorious fellowship with his heavenly Father, felt abandoned. This was when he cried out, *"My God, my God, why have you forsaken me?"* Jesus, the beloved of the Father, bore our sins, died in our place, took on himself the wrath we deserved, and experienced separation from the Father and the darkness of hell.

Why? We must ask this question again. Why would Jesus willingly walk into a world that would assault and abuse him physically? Why would he keep loving sinful people when we rejected him? Why would Jesus allow himself to bear our sin, take the wrath of God, and experience the darkness of hellish separation from his Father?

The answer echoes through history. Jesus had a mission. His mission was you. His mission was me. We were the lost sheep Jesus came to find. He decided, before the foundation of the world, that we were worth the sacrifice: his own life.

Our Call

We do not need to be powerful and come up with some clever new source of meaning, adventure, and purpose in life. We are not powerless and consigned to a meaningless existence. Those who have been found by Jesus are empowered to join his mission. We are invited to walk with the risen Lord Jesus, filled with his Holy Spirit, as we share the love of the Father with a broken and lost world. Our mission is to join our God in his continuing quest to seek and save the lost.

There is no mission more meaningful. There is nothing more exciting!

To live as Jesus lived, love as he loved, and share the good news as he did will demand more than we have. We must be empowered by his presence. As this happens, we will receive the strength we need to accomplish his mission for us.

His mission will become ours. His heart will beat in our chest. His love will flow freely through us. The world will see the presence of the risen and glorious Lord of the universe and find in him the hope, grace, and power that only he can bring.

From the Heart of Jesus

Dear Partner in the Mission,

The call to seek and save lost people is not yet completed. You walk past men and women every day who desperately need the grace, truth, and strength of Jesus. They are broken, hurting, empty, and often don't even know it.

If you have received forgiveness for your sins, new life, and friendship with God, you have a mission. Pass on what you have freely received. Let the world know, in your own way, that God freely offers the gift of salvation to anyone who receives the grace of Jesus.

Let the mission of Jesus become your consuming passion. Wake up every day and before your feet hit the floor pray, "Lord, send me out into this day with a heart like yours. Use me to extend your love and share your gospel with those who are lost. Empower me for this great calling. Pour me out. Use me for your glory! Amen!"

▸▸ **Walk with Jesus** and learn more about powerfully following the will of the Father and his mission by reading Luke 19; John 3 and 4.

Resources for Living an Empowered Life

Receiving the Strength You Need Today

When God is near and we live in his presence, his heart becomes our heart. The mission of God is to reach people who are wandering far from him, like sheep without a shepherd. As we become more like Jesus and grow in maturity, our heart breaks for the things that break the heart of God. On the top of the list is people. God longs to reach those who still need his love, healing, hope, grace, and friendship. One of the primary ways God has always accomplished his plan of reaching the world with the good news of Jesus is through ordinary people.

If we want to be empowered to live for God in this world, one of the best ways is for us to enter into his mission, follow his call, and organize our days around his purposes. As we do this, we will have a reason to get out of bed in the morning. There will be a driving force that propels us through each day. We will go to bed each night excited and praying for God to lead us into the adventure of another day. Few things empower a follower of Jesus more than living on mission with the will and plans of God!

Here are some ideas, prayers, and activities that can help you experience God's power as you follow God's will for your life and accomplish his mission in this world.

Daily Reading Guide for Week 4 of *Empowered*

Use these daily Bible readings and chapters from *Empowered* to gain a solid biblical picture of people who have experienced being empowered through following God's mission and call on their life. Learn and be inspired as you enter into their story.

Day and Character	Bible Reading	Reading in *Empowered*
Day 1—Paul's Call	Acts 9 and 26	Chapter 19
Day 2—Isaiah's Invitation	Isaiah 6	Chapter 20
Day 3—Abraham's Journey	Genesis 12:1–9 and Genesis 17	Chapter 21
Day 4—Esther's Risk	Esther 2–4	Chapter 22
Day 5—Mary's Maternity	Luke 1:1–56 and 2:1–40	Chapter 23
Weekend—Jesus's Mission	Luke 19	Chapter 24

Prayer Guide

Take time to pray using the following prompts and ask God to empower you in fresh new ways:

- Thank God that when you were heading in the wrong direction and still far from him, he loved and called you.
- Confess where you still tend to wander and head in the wrong direction and ask for the power of the Holy Spirit to help you repent and follow God's will and mission for your life with greater faithfulness.
- Ask God to give you boldness to follow his calling and plan for your life even when you don't have all the details figured out.
- Pray for courage to take risks for God and to follow him even when the consequences could be costly.

- Thank Jesus for serving you through his life and death and pray to be empowered as his servant each and every day.
- Ask the Holy Spirit to help you identify people who are lost and wandering far from him. Pray for your heart to go out to these people and for strength to reach out to them with the love, grace, and message of Jesus.

Journal and Personal Reflections

Write some of your own thoughts and reflections on the following topics and questions:

What was my life like before following Jesus? What were the signs that I was heading in the wrong direction?

How does my life become more meaningful, rich, and fruitful as I identify God's mission and follow it?

What are signs that we live among a people of unclean lips (as Isaiah said)? What are specific ways you can stay pure and holy in a world that has so much sin?

_____

_____

_____

_____

_____

When was a time you really took a bold risk as you followed God's will? How did God use your faithfulness to accomplish something that brought him glory?

_____

_____

_____

_____

When is it most difficult for you to have a servant's heart and to enter into humble acts of service? What is one act of service you could do this week that would really stretch you?

_____

_____

_____

_____

Action Ideas

Use one or more of the following ideas or exercises to plug into God's power in the coming days:

Trajectory Study

Write four or five words, sentences, brief paragraphs that describe the trajectory of your life before you placed your faith in Jesus.

Next, write four or five words, sentences, brief paragraphs that describe where you are in your walk of faith right now. Be honest and vulnerable with yourself and with God.

Then, write four or five words, sentences, brief paragraphs that describe where you believe God wants you to head in your life and faith. These should reflect his mission for you and will for your life.

Set two or three specific goals to help you align the trajectory of your life to match where you know God wants you to head. Ask a few trusted friends to pray for you and keep you accountable to pursue these actions and attitudes that will set you on a course to fulfill God's will for you.

Life Mission Statement

Jesus declared:

For the Son of Man came to seek and to save the lost. (Luke 19:10)

The apostle Paul said:

I have become all things to all people so that by all possible means I might save some. I do all this for the sake of the gospel, that I may share in its blessings. (1 Cor. 9:22–23)

I (Kevin Harney) have no question that God has placed me on this planet to do two things:

*Reach the lost **and** teach the found to reach the lost.*

Take some time to prayerfully consider what you believe God has called you to do with your life. As a follower of Jesus you are called to let his light shine through you. You are his witness. In your own words, seek to crystallize your calling and mission in this world.

_____

_____

_____

_____

_____

Afterword

Receiving the Strength I Need Today

Strength for today. All of us need it.

The only true lasting source of power for our lives is found in the presence of the God who made the universe. His reservoir is endless. He is willing and waiting to infuse us with his strength. All we have to do is draw near to him and allow him to fill us.

How will God do this? Now there is the question.

In ways we might not expect.

God's empowering presence is found in moments of *suffering, loss, and pain*. We don't invite these moments or seasons, but they do come. In these times of desperation, God draws near and fills us with strength we could never experience on our own.

Our heavenly Father places us in a family of faith. When we live in the presence of Jesus and receive his grace, we are placed in a *community* of people God uses to strengthen us. We don't walk alone, but God surrounds us with brothers and sisters in Christ who become conduits of heavenly encouragement, blessing, and empowerment.

The Lord of the Sabbath calls us to *rest*, rejuvenate, and be replenished. We tend to run hard, resist slowing down, and push forward in our own power. God wants to empower us through a rhythm of rest that punctuates our days and weeks.

As we wake up each morning, we can be propelled forward, energized to live for God, as we hear his *call* and follow his *mission* for our life.

Don't try to be powerful in your own strength. Your reserves will run out faster than you can imagine.

Don't live a powerless life, believing that God can't use you or work through you.

Invite God to *empower* you each day. Stay close to Jesus. Live in his presence. Let him fill you with the strength you need today, tomorrow, and every day of your life.

Small Group Discussion Guide

Jesus knew the importance of small groups. He gathered with people at meals, around tables, walking through the open country, in quiet gardens, and in private homes. Jesus loved being with small groups of people for the express purpose of learning, mutual encouragement, and spiritual refreshment. He designed his ministry around a small group—twelve imperfect, passionate, struggling disciples. One of the Savior's most common tools for helping his followers grow was asking them questions that caused them to reflect, struggle, and take action.

What follows are reflection questions designed to help you think deeply, act wisely, and learn together as a group. Be sure to use the DVD teaching content and stories. The DVD can be purchased on the Baker website (bakerpublishinggroup.com) or on the keving harney.com website. The DVD teaching, small group questions, and biblical readings will work together to create an experience of learning, mutual accountability, and life application. My prayer is that the Holy Spirit will show up each time your group gathers and lead you to a place of God-ordained empowerment!

In Joy,
Kevin G. Harney

Session 1

Experiencing God's Presence in Suffering, Loss, and Pain

▶ **Watch**: "Introduction to *Empowered*" on the *Empowered* DVD

1. How have you seen people (yourself or others) seek to be powerful and self-assured when they should actually be looking to God for empowerment? What are some possible consequences of looking to ourselves to be powerful instead of relying on God?

2. How have you seen people (yourself or others) feeling powerless and out of control? What are some possible consequences when a person believes they are powerless and there is no hope for them to get out of their circumstances?

▶ **Watch**: "Session 1—Experiencing God's Presence in Suffering, Loss, and Pain" on the *Empowered* DVD

3. Tell a story of a Christian you have watched go through a time of hardship, suffering, or loss and describe how God was with them and empowered them along the way.

Pain, loss, and struggle can
become a conduit of God's grace
and power in our lives.

Read: 2 Corinthians 11:23–28 and 12:7–10

4. The apostle Paul was being faithful in following Jesus, he was fulfilling God's purpose and mission for his life. But, he still faced great hardship, loss, and pain. What was Paul's

attitude toward his sufferings and what can we learn from his example?

5. In the DVD, Hasan says, "I know that God was with me through the toughest time in my life." How have you met God and been empowered by him as you have faced difficult times of pain and loss?

6. In the DVD, Hasan explains that he wants to protect his daughter from the pain of the world. But, he also realizes that he does not want to overprotect her because God will empower her and draw near her in the struggles we all face walking through life. What are some of the rich spiritual lessons and experiences of God's presence we can miss if we try to avoid all pain and struggles in life?

7. Share a lesson of empowerment through suffering that you have learned through your reading of section one of the book or the Bible passages provided for your reading. Tell about one of the characters (Job, Paul, Hannah, Joseph, Peter, or Jesus) and how their journey has impacted your life.

8. What are ways your small group members can help show the presence, love, and empowering presence of Jesus to each other in times of struggle, pain, and loss that other group members might face?

"We have to go through those times to be refined. God is there in the tough times. . . . He'll always bring you through."

—Hasan Houston

211

9. What is one specific way your group members can support, encourage, and minister the empowering presence of Jesus to another group member in the coming weeks?

10. What specific ways can you be praying for each other from today until the next time you meet?

Session 2

Encountering God in the Community of His People

1. Tell about some of the different expressions of Christian community that you experience in the flow of a normal month. How do you meet and encounter God in these various relational connections? CHURCH, SMALL GROUP, MEETING WITH ACCOUNTABILITY PARTNER

▶ Watch: "Session 2—Encountering God in the Community of His People" on the *Empowered* DVD

2. Tell about a godly Christian person the Lord has placed in your life to help strengthen you and give guidance as you grow on your journey with Jesus. GEORGE BERNING

"I have felt God taking my hand through my grandmother in pretty much every interaction I have ever had with her since I can remember."

—Robin Smitherman

Read: Matthew 26:36–39; Luke 8:51–56; and Matthew 17:1–6

212

3. At critical times of his life and ministry, Jesus gathered three close friends around him. What do you learn from this rhythm in the life of Jesus and how can we follow his example of building community and letting others come close to us?

God exists in eternal community!

4. In the DVD story you meet four people who are both a family by blood and by faith in Jesus. Marian Piña is Roy's mother. Roy Piña is Robin's father. Robin Smitherman is Crystal's mother. Four generations seeking to walk in community together. Robin talks about longing to take what she has learned from her parents and grandmother and pass it on to the next generation. Why is it critical and essential that we all seek to pass on faith in Jesus to the next generation? What are practical ways we can do this?

Read: 1 Timothy 1:1–2

5. Who is one person that has acted as a spiritual parent in your life and how has God used them to help you experience his presence and to empower you?

6. Who is one person God has placed in your life who you feel the call to invest in and help grow in faith? How can God use you to help this person feel his presence and power?

7. Share a lesson of empowerment through community that you have learned through your reading of section two of the book or the Bible passages provided for your reading. Tell about one of the relationships that impacted you (the paralytic and his friends, Paul and Timothy, Ruth and Naomi, Lois . . . Eunice . . . and Timothy, the woman at the well, Jesus and

his friends). How has their journey influenced and inspired you to grow in community?

8. What are ways your small group members can extend deeper community to each other so that each of you can see God more clearly and feel his care more personally?

One of the greatest sources of power for your life, day by day, is to stay connected in great and godly relationships.

Session 3

Empowered for the Journey by Receiving God's Rest

1. Tell about a time when your schedule was intensely full, the demands of your life were growing, and you found yourself not getting the rest, refreshment, and time for revitalization that you needed. How did the demands of this season of life and the lack of rest impact you in some of the different parts of your life (physically, spiritually, emotionally, relationally . . .)?

▶ Watch: "Session 3—Empowered for the Journey by Receiving God's Rest" on the *Empowered* DVD

2. What are some of the things that drive us to push ourselves to the point of exhaustion and refuse to find space for rest and refreshment?

Empowered people have found an amazing
balance of working hard and resting well!

3. In the DVD, Rick tells about a serious wake-up call that forced
him to face his own limitations, mortality, and need to dial
back and make space for rest and refreshment. Tell about a
time when you faced the reality that you are not a machine
and that you need to learn to unplug, breathe deep, slow
down, and find the refreshment that God designed you to
need. How did you adjust your lifestyle after this experience?

"I can be a much more effective father,
husband, physician, and friend with
adequate rest."

—Dr. Rick Alexander

Read: Isaiah 30:15–18; Psalm 127:1–2; Exodus 20:8–11; and Matthew 11:28–30

4. Why do you think God is so serious about his children learning to rest and find places of quiet and refreshment?

5. How is your spiritual life and intimacy with God impacted
when you are driven, busy, and pushing past your normal limitations? What are some specific ways we can build a rhythm
of rest and refreshment into our lives so we can connect with
God deeply and consistently?

Read: Genesis 2:2–3

6. God is all-powerful, he sustains the universe, and he never gets tired. Why do you think God took a Sabbath day of rest? If God rested as an example for his children, how do you think he feels when we resist taking a day off, slowing down, and enjoying the refreshment he offers?

> We can get more done in six days
> of labor and a good day of rest,
> than in seven days of work!

Read: Mark 1:35

7. Jesus made space to pull away from the demands of life and meet quietly with the Father. How does this become a model and example for us? What do you do, in the rhythm of your day and week, to make space to be quiet with God and receive his rest and empowerment?

8. Share a lesson of empowerment through rest and refreshment that you have learned through your reading of section three of the book or the Bible passages provided for your reading. Tell about one of the biblical stories that impacted you (God's day off, Moses's teaching on Sabbath, Israel's struggle, Psalm 23, Elijah's nap, and Jesus's early mornings). How does this passage challenge you to develop disciplines?

9. What is one practical step you can take to build a rhythm of rest and Sabbath into your life and how can your group members pray for you and keep you accountable to live this out?

Session 4

Propelled Onward by the Call and Mission of God

1. Tell about a time you sensed God's call or leading in your life. How did this clarify your awareness of God's vision for your life?

▶ **Watch**: "Session 4—Propelled Onward by the Call and Mission of God" on the *Empowered* DVD

2. In the DVD story you learned about how Sherry finished an advanced theology class and said to herself, "I am glad I will never have to take another class like that." Years later, God called her to undertake a Master's degree in theology. Tell about a time when God called you to do something that surprised, stretched, or even scared you. How did your faith deepen as you followed God on this journey?

3. What are some of the ways God speaks to us and directs us toward his mission for our life? How can we get ourselves in a posture and place where we can hear from God and grow in confidence that we are following his call for our life?

In my heart I heard God say this very clearly: "Do you want to be in my will?" And I answered, "Yes Lord, I want to be in your will."

—Sherry Harney

Read: Isaiah 6:1–8

4. What prepared Isaiah to hear and follow God's call? How did Isaiah respond to the leading and mission of God?

Read: Genesis 12:1–5

5. What do you learn as you watch Abraham following God with limited instructions and details? What helps you follow God, even when you don't have the whole trip mapped out in advance?

God wants to give you a mission. He wants to call you as you read his Word, as you listen to his Holy Spirit, and as you walk in community with his people.

6. How has following the mission and call of God on your life brought greater joy, deeper meaning, or a more profound connection with Jesus?

7. Share a lesson of empowerment through God's clarifying call to a life mission that you have learned as you read section three of the book or the Bible passages provided for your reading. Tell about one of the biblical stories of being called to a mission that impacted you (Paul, Isaiah, Abraham, Esther, Mary, or Jesus). How did this story inspire you to listen for God's call and follow his mission for your life?

8. Tell your small group about some call or mission of God that you have felt called to follow but have not yet acted on. How can they pray for you, encourage you, and keep you accountable to take a next step of obedience toward this mission?

Notes

Chapter 1: Job's Epic Story of Suffering

1. Jerry Sittser's book, *A Grace Disguised: How the Soul Grows through Loss* (Grand Rapids: Zondervan, 1995, 2004), tells the story in powerful detail.
2. See Job 1:18–19.

Chapter 2: Paul's 195 Scars

1. Acts 1:8.

Chapter 3: Hannah's Sorrow and Tears

1. See 1 Samuel 1:8.
2. See 1 Samuel 1:6.
3. 1 Samuel 1:17.
4. See 1 Samuel 1:11.

Chapter 4: Joseph's Journey of Loss

1. In his book *Twelve Years a Slave*, first published in 1853, Solomon Northup gives a detailed account of all he experienced during his slavery. He reports details from the treatment of slaves to the process of picking cotton, to the attitudes of slave owners. It is a powerful and chilling account of how human beings can treat each other with utter disregard.
2. Genesis 39:21.
3. See Genesis 40:14.
4. Genesis 39:2–5, 21, 23.
5. See Genesis 45:4–7 and 50:15–21

Chapter 5: Peter, a Disciple's Sacrifice

1. My book *Reckless Faith* (Grand Rapids: Baker, 2012) will help you explore the call to full and radical discipleship.
2. Matthew 4:18–19.
3. Mark 10:28.
4. See the Acts of Peter XXXVII: "I beseech you the executioners, crucify me thus, with the head downward and not otherwise: and the reason wherefore, I will tell unto them that hear"; http://www.earlychristianwritings.com/text/actspeter.html; also, *Ecclesiastical History of Eusebius Pamphilius*, book III, chap. I: "At last, having come to Rome, he was crucified head-downwards; for he had requested that he might suffer in this way"; http://www.preteristarchive.com/

ChurchHistory/0325_eusebius_history
.html.

Chapter 6: Jesus's Scream of Loneliness

1. See Matthew 26:69–75.
2. See Luke 22:61.
3. See Matthew 21:9 and 27:22.
4. 2 Corinthians 5:21.

Chapter 8: Paul and Timothy

1. See Acts 9 and 11.
2. 2 Timothy 1:2; Acts 16:1–4; Philippians 2:19–24.

Chapter 9: Ruth and Naomi

1. See Ruth 1:1.
2. Ruth 1:3.
3. Ruth 1:5.
4. See Matthew 1:5.

Chapter 10: Lois, Eunice, and Timothy

1. See Luke 15.
2. The word *Shema* means "Hear." It is the first word of Deuteronomy 6:4 in the Hebrew version.

Chapter 11: The Woman at the Well

1. See John 4:9.
2. William Barclay's commentary on the Gospel of John goes into the history of this conflict between the Jews and Samaritans in great detail.
3. Let Us Reason website, article on "Women in the Biblical Times."
4. John 4:39.

Chapter 12: Jesus and His Friends

1. Matthew 26:38.
2. See Luke 22:44.
3. See Luke 22:47.

Chapter 13: God's Example

1. See Mark 2:23–28.
2. In chapter 7 of my book *Seismic Shifts* (Grand Rapids: Zondervan, 2005), I address the topic of Sabbath in great detail and have a section of FAQs on this topic if you want to dig deeper into it.

Chapter 14: Moses's Teaching

1. See Genesis 15:13.
2. Exodus 19:5–6.
3. See Exodus 19.
4. See chap. 13, "God's Example."
5. Proverbs 27:17.
6. See Matthew 22:37–40.

Chapter 15: Israel's Struggle

1. See Exodus 16:2.
2. See Exodus 16.
3. See Exodus 16:20.
4. See Exodus 16:22.

Chapter 16: David's Shepherd Psalm

1. See 1 Samuel 17:34–36.
2. See 1 Peter 5:8.
3. See John 10:1–21.

Chapter 17: Elijah's Turning Point

1. 1 Kings 19:2.
2. 1 Kings 19:3.
3. See 1 Kings 19:3–4.
4. See 1 Kings 19:5–6.
5. 1 Kings 19:7.

Chapter 18: Jesus's Early Mornings

1. See Mark 1:21–38.
2. In the first six chapters of my book *Seismic Shifts*, I walk through ways Christians can grow in their daily walk and friendship with God.
3. See Mark 1:38.

4. Two of Juan Carlos's most famous books are *Disciple* (Orlando, FL: Creation House, 1995) and *Call to Discipleship* (Plainfield, NJ: Logos International, 1975).

Chapter 19: Paul's Call

1. See Acts 7:58.
2. See Acts 6:1–6.
3. See Acts 8:1.
4. See Acts 22:1–5.
5. Acts 22:4.
6. See 1 Timothy 1:15.
7. See 1 Timothy 1:16.

Chapter 20: Isaiah's Invitation

1. 2 Chronicles 26:4.
2. Isaiah 6:3.
3. Isaiah 6:5.
4. Isaiah 6:7.
5. Isaiah 6:8a.
6. Isaiah 6:8b.
7. Matthew 28:19–20.
8. Acts 1:8.

Chapter 21: Abraham's Journey

1. See Genesis 12:1–3.
2. Genesis 12:7 (emphasis mine).
3. See Genesis 12:7.
4. In the book *Reckless Faith*, I write about living the adventure of following Jesus and taking up the cross every day of our life.

5. Matthew 4:19.
6. Matthew 4:22.
7. Luke 9:23–24.

Chapter 22: Esther's Risk

1. See Esther 1:12.
2. See Esther 1:12–22.
3. See Esther 2:1–18.
4. See Esther 3:8–15.
5. See Esther 4.

Chapter 23: Mary's Maternity

1. See Luke 1:26–38.
2. See Matthew 1:1–17.

Chapter 24: Jesus's Mission

1. See Romans 8:34.
2. See Philippians 2:5–11.
3. See Revelation 13:8.
4. See Mark 3:20–21.
5. See Matthew 12:24.
6. Matthew 21:9.
7. Matthew 27:22.
8. See Matthew 26:56.
9. See Matthew 26:69–75.
10. See Matthew 26:14–16.
11. See Matthew 26:53.
12. A Roman legion had 6,000 soldiers.
13. See Romans 5:9–10 and Hebrews 2:17.

Kevin G. Harney (MDiv, Fuller Seminary; DMin, Western Theological Seminary) is lead pastor of Shoreline Community Church in Monterey, California. He also serves as the visionary leader of the Organic Outreach Organization (a movement designed to move local churches into the world with the gospel). Harney is the author of many books, including *Reckless Faith* and the *Organic Outreach* series, as well as small group studies, curriculum, and articles. He also does extensive teaching and speaking both nationally and internationally.

4-WEEK VIDEO SERIES

- Session 1: Experiencing God's Presence in Suffering, Loss, and Pain

- Session 2: Encountering God in the Community of His People

- Session 3: Empowered for the Journey by Receiving God's Rest

- Session 4: Propelled Onward by the Call and Mission of God

Visit **KevinGHarney.com** for **FREE** *Empowered by His Presence* Extras:

- » Small Group Resources
- » Preaching Resources and Ideas
- » Bible Reading Schedule
- » And more

BakerBooks

BakerBooks.com
Available wherever books and ebooks are sold.

FOLLOWING GOD HAS ALWAYS BEEN RISKY.
BUT GOD DOESN'T WANT US TO PLAY IT SAFE.

This energizing book challenges you to count the cost, take a chance, and live a reckless faith for the entire world to see. With a focus on "responsible recklessness," Kevin Harney shows you how to develop a high-impact lifestyle that is supported by prayer, wisdom, the direction of Scripture, and insightful counsel from other believers. Through *Reckless Faith*, you'll discover how to be reckless in your love, generosity, service, relationships, and prayers.

NOW IN PAPER

Visit **KevinGHarney.com** for more *Reckless Faith* resources

BakerBooks
BakerBooks.com
Available wherever books and ebooks are sold.